FLAT ASS CALM

A MEMOIR

AMY M. MCMULLEN

Published 2017 by

MCAIMLESS PUBLISHING, LLC

Phoenix, Arizona

Copyright © 2017 Amy M. McMullen

Color Edition

ISBN 978-09996171-0-6

For Orca and Kila

FLAT ASS CALM

.

TABLE OF CONTENTS

PREFACE

Everything contained in these pages is as is close to the truth as I could make it. But while my memory may be prodigious, it's not photographic; therefore, the dialogue will approximate what was actually said, and the timeline may be a tiny bit crooked here and there.

This memoir covers my life from the 1950s to the early 1980s. It's a long time ago, and if others think they remember these events differently, they're welcome to write about them from their own perspective. This, however, is how I remember it.

Some things I describe are neither pleasant nor flattering, whether for myself or others depicted. I've changed many of the names in order to keep as much distance as possible from those who I assume had no wish to be included. My goal was for this work to be honest, perhaps even brutally so. The passage of time has a way of erasing our histories, unless someone bothers to write them down. So that is what I've done, and this is my story.

Amy M. McMullen

FLAT ASS CALM

PART I

FLAT ASS CALM

CHAPTER ONE ~ HIJACKED DREAMS

I am a rock. I am an island.
But a rock is never sad,
And an island never cries.

—Paul Simon

If you happen to be floating around in the Gulf of Maine at any point in your life, keep an eye out for two small islands huddled together far off the coast. They're just a couple of lonely bumps of land surrounded by deep water, and together they resemble a whale rising from the sea. They don't have many people living on them, but they'll lure you in if you're easily seduced by rough cliffs, silent woods, or an old village encrusted with a thick layer of salt.

Be very careful of these islands; they've been known to snare the unwary. They hijacked my dreams once, and I was never the same again.

***

The indigenous Kennebec people named the two islands Monhegan, (Big Island), and Manana, (Little Island). They sit in the Gulf of Maine—about ten miles from the nearest mainland—and were once the bumpy summit of an ancient mountain, created out of fire and geologic upheaval. As millennia marched by, glaciers advanced then retreated, leaving behind rounded hilltops surrounded by a sea of melted ice.

The islands were first inhabited by local native tribes as a summer fishing ground, later settled by European and British colonizers who battled the harsh winters but stayed year-round. The Europeans were lured by the almighty codfish, easily plucked from the cold waters, dried by the thousands, packed in salt, and sent back across the Atlantic to feed the teeming masses. These hardy souls persevered for generations, battling the elements, building wooden shacks and houses, and cutting down all the islands' trees for firewood.

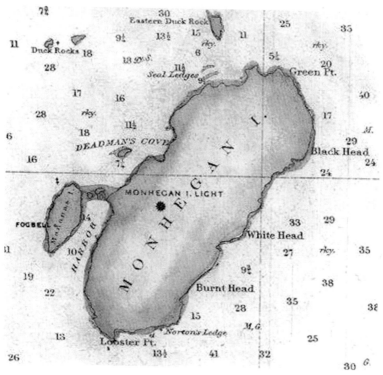

Manana and Monhegan Islands (United States Coast Survey, 1864 Edition)

Long before the arrival of white people, lobsters were so plentiful on the Maine coast that they would wash up by the thousands in drifts on the shore. Native Americans would scoop the brown crustaceans out of tide pools to use as fishing bait and fertilizer. The earliest colonists took advantage of the abundance of lobsters, and even adopted the Natives' disparaging attitude that they were barely edible.

Through the mid-nineteenth century, lobster was used as a poverty food, to be fed to indentured servants, enslaved people, and prisoners. Local legend claims there was a "lobster rebellion" among indentured servants during the 1700s, forcing a contractual agreement that limited servings of "cockroaches of the sea" to a maximum of three times per week. With the advent of canning and improved distribution with railroads, the "trash fish" became a cheap popular food to be shipped across the country; by World War II, the lowly lobster was finally elevated to its rightful place as a luxury item.

Always of a mind to take advantage of gastronomic trends, Monhegan's inhabitants quickly began setting wooden traps on the rocky ocean bottom and hauling in flapping, snapping lobsters to sell to mainlanders. The boats used by the island fishermen to ply their seafaring trade were tied to moorings that littered the harbor between the two islands: first sloops, schooners, and dories, then internal combustion-driven lobster boats, fishing smacks, and seine boats.

Sometime during the nineteenth century, Monhegan also became a haven for summer visitors. Wealthy Bostonians and New Yorkers took steamships up the coast, fleeing disease-ridden cities to keep their children safe and healthy in the clean salt air. Then artists took notice of the rugged beauty and flocked to the island to set up studios and paint endless seascapes. Finally, by the late nineteenth century, tourism arrived; soon thousands of people touring the Maine coast could jump on a ferry and spend the day, or a few nights, or a whole summer on the island. The summer population quintupled, and little summer homes and inns dotted the landscape.

Over the centuries, only Monhegan was inhabited year-round, while Manana hosted a foghorn station, some sheep, and an occasional hermit or two. During the late 1970s, my husband and I lived on Manana, which was accessible only by hard rowing across a harbor open to the southwesterly seas, frequently fraught with foul weather and towering waves during the winter. The landing on our shore was nothing but rocks—a dark gray, densely grained granite that formed the bones of the island. These rocks were covered with slick seaweed, except at the highest tide, and continuously washed by a restless sea. The entire island was just one big hundred-acre rock that rose from the water to form an egg-shaped hump with almost perpendicular sides, a tough turf skin, and one lonely tree.

Rockwell Kent (1882-1971) "Afternoon on the Sea, Monhegan" 1907

At first glance I thought Manana was a bleak prospect; grasses, mosses, thistle, a few wind-tortured bushes, with a spine of bedrock jutting up through the thin soil. There were also the many strange piles of small rocks, obviously formed by human hands, which dotted the landscape. They seemed to serve no purpose. It was far too easy to reach the conclusion that Manana was simply a lonely, windy, and uninhabitable rock. But if I looked closely, I could see beauty amidst the harshness: tiny white wildflowers and sweet wild strawberries peeking out from the turf in the summertime; cranberries in the little bog, like red jewels in the autumn, where carnivorous sundew plants also lurked, waiting patiently to snare an unwary insect with a sweet trap of death; or the boundless ocean, with the mainland glimmering on a far-off horizon.

I would spy on the nesting gulls along the shore ledges; they believed their nurseries were safe from marauders and fed their wheedling, downy tan babies without reacting to my presence. I would eagerly seek out the excitement of schooling mackerel ripping the water with their mysterious dance, and sighing minke whales creasing the surface nearby.

There were deep scratches in a ledge of rock on top of the island that were once thought to be Norse or Phoenician inscriptions. These inscriptions also resembled the marks that might have been made by a prehistoric rock caught between a glacier and a hard place. But they drew many who came to ponder their possibilities and run fingers in the ancient grooves.

"Norse" Inscriptions – Manana (Bob McMullen)

The water was cold; in winter the temperature of the salty ocean can drop below 32°F and even at more moderate times of year, humans could not bear the frigidness for long. A trip overboard was a flirtation with hypothermia, but the seeds of self-preservation had no firm root in me or my husband. We took outrageous risks crossing the harbor, since the possibilities of death and disaster simply did not exist in our minds.

It was all a matter of timing: wait for the wave to come in, then hurry, hurry, rush the skiff down the sloping granite, stern-first, into the water before the wave retreated. You had to jump into the boat and ride out in a giddy rush, hoping that a rock wouldn't catch the bottom and hang you sideways in the wash, where you would be helpless to the next wave, oars flung from the oarlocks, bailer and maybe yourself—washed into the frigid waters.

I became a strong rower. Submerged rocks near Manana made the use of an outboard motor impractical, and engines required endless maintenance and tinkering to keep working. By contrast, the oars were extensions of my arms, slicing and catching the water with habitual precision, feathering perfectly on the forward stroke, propelling the bow strongly forward on the backward pull. I could row facing forward and pushing, or facing backward and pulling. My husband and I made crossings with barely enough freeboard to stay above water, and always, always, our little boat leaked. Repeated landings on rocks are not good for skiffs, and boat repairs were a frequent and necessary fact of life.

Rowing my toddler across the harbor

I nonchalantly carried our babies on my back; rowing us across that strait without so much as a single life jacket on board during weather that anyone with half a brain could see was dangerous. Instead of ending up a sad footnote in the island's history, we survived, due entirely, I believe, to luck.

People on Monhegan talked about us. We were the hermits: alternately admired, ridiculed, chastised, and encouraged—minor celebrities of a sort. For my husband this made it all worthwhile. The gossip embarrassed me, and I didn't enjoy the attention. I was a teenage bride completely under the influence of a charismatic young man, eight years my senior; a man who had strong and absolute ideas of right and wrong and how our lives would be lived. To disagree with him was to risk alienation or worse, and that was too great a price to pay. For the privilege of this peculiar existence I had already walked away from my fragmented family, leaving them fearing for my safety. My pride did not allow me to go back, so I was adrift; my only anchor was the tempestuous marriage I had fallen into, with its bipolar extremes of happiness and despair.

FLAT ASS CALM

CHAPTER TWO ~ MANANA

We live on a placid island of ignorance in the midst of black seas of infinity, and it was not meant that we should voyage far.

--H. P. Lovecraft

We moved to Manana during the summer of 1976. The island had formerly been inhabited by a man named Ray Phillips, who had lived there since the 1930s, eking out a hardscrabble existence on that lonely rock. His only companions were his flock of sheep and a pet goose named Donald.

Ray was the Hermit of Manana—straight out of central casting with a shaggy beard, a pipe of foul-smelling tobacco clenched in his few remaining teeth, and a sweet demeanor. He was enveloped in the overpowering odor of sheep, because the man rarely, if ever, bathed.

Ray spent much of his time moving all the loose rocks on Manana into piles. People assumed that he began doing this to clear the grass for his sheep, but it became an obsession that went beyond practicality, resulting in a spine so hunched that he was bent double in his later years.

The Hermit of Manana died alone in his shack one winter night and his sheep were removed from the island not long after. Donald the goose remained, and we bought a mate for him during our first winter on Monhegan. They produced a gosling in the early spring that—since the weather was still cold and inhospitable for such a fragile creature—I raised by hand, carrying her in my backpack until she was large enough to waddle behind me. Our goose was soon joined by goats, chickens, more sheep, ducks, pigs, rabbits, and a braying strawberry roan donkey we named Jacques Derriere.

The Hermit of Manana (Joe Votano collection)

We occupied the hermit's home: a wacky assortment of shacks built out of discarded lumber, pieces of an old boat, and driftwood. It was haphazardly tied together by lopsided walkways and crazy rooflines, all clinging precariously to the nearly vertical side of the island. There was no electricity, phone, or running water. There wasn't even a well, only a very green pool at the top of the island—used as a bathtub by the gulls—and gutters off our roof for catching rainwater.

The first time I visited these buildings was in 1975, with my then-boyfriend, Thomas. He excitedly showed me through the rooms, all the while drawing fantastic verbal pictures of wondrous possibilities.

But honestly, what impressed me most about the place was the sheep shit. The hermit had quite literally lived with his animals and there was manure—three to six inches deep—on all the floors. The walls were black with smoke from his fires and pipes; the place stank of muck, decay, and the sad memories of his departed presence.

Ray Phillips cutting hay on Monhegan (Lorimer Brackett)

Scattered everywhere were small pieces of the old man's life: a broken briar pipe here, a little crockery there, tattered rags of clothing, and a totally incongruous, white-enameled bathtub, half-filled with sheep dung.

Rumor had it that at some point, Ray had decided to get married and, in anticipation of having a feminine presence in the house, went inshore to purchase plumbing fixtures. He painstakingly hauled a bathtub, sink, and toilet over to his home, only to have them sit unused and unattached for decades, since no willing bride was forthcoming. Anyway, there wasn't a water source to run them.

That night, after my first tour of the house on Manana, we camped out on that little island. We trekked to the top of the steep hill, where the view across the harbor was of Monhegan, spread out before us—a tiny village with little toy boats bobbing in the harbor. After unrolling our sleeping bags on the softest moss imaginable, we lay watching the brilliant stars move overhead. Before I drifted off to sleep I thought, yes... I could live here.

Before we moved in, we had to spend many hours on our hands and knees scraping the multitudinous layers of crap off the floors. Our arms ached from sweeping generations of spider webs out of the rafters; it was a daunting task to make the place even minimally habitable. We constructed a loft for sleeping, and in one room, we assembled a kitchen, consisting of a gas hot plate, a sink that drained onto the ground on the other side of the wall, and an old wood cook stove. We concluded that Ray Phillips had existed entirely on baby food and cottage cheese because we had to dispose of hundreds of jars and cartons of both, all with rotted traces of their original contents.

We built a privy of stone in one of the attached buildings and collected rainwater in garbage cans. We insulated two rooms for us to live in; the rest were left for the animals. Thomas knew how to weld, so he assembled a wood stove out of old propane cylinders and poked the stovepipe with its shanty cap through a hole in the roof.

Hermit Shacks on Manana (Abby Sewall)

It was a home of gray wood, kerosene fumes, wood smoke, summer flies, dripping roofs, and an endless battle against dirt and cold. Every stick of wood, bag of food, gallon of kerosene, or tank of propane had to be rowed across the harbor in a leaky skiff, wrestled out onto a rock landing—often between relentless gusting waves—and carried one hundred feet up an incredibly steep hill to this house.

We finally obtained permission from the hermit's surviving sister to rent the buildings for a pittance shortly before our first child was born. The permission had taken some time to secure because she worried that we would become squatters and challenge her ownership of the portion she had inherited. The island itself was divided into shares with no surveyed boundaries. Aside from a couple of men stationed at the small Coast Guard foghorn station, we were the only inhabitants.

View of Monhegan from Manana Island, ca. early 1900s (Penobscot Marine Museum)

I went along willingly. To survive my rocky childhood, I had developed a stubborn nature that pitted me against all obstacles. The stark beauty of Manana charmed me, and I knew that with time, I would be able to accept the daunting inconveniences of daily life. Most importantly, however, I was madly in love with Thomas and would follow him to the moon.

Despite our desire for isolation, we both found that we also craved society. Our lives were dictated by frequent trips across the harbor to Monhegan. We would go on the pretense of getting our mail or having a shower at his parents' house we called the "Summer Cottage." We would loiter at the Periwinkle Coffee Shop for hours to chat with friends, or would hang out at some party. Our needs contradicted themselves; the desire to be isolated, heroic homesteaders competed with our daily need for company and friends.

Launching off the rocks

In the wintertime our harbor crossings were limited by necessity to the days that the mail boat came to Monhegan: Mondays, Wednesdays, and Fridays. We prayed for good weather on those days, but calm crossings were a rare occurrence in the winter. In preparation for our trips across the harbor, I would bundle up our baby in layers, cover the layers with snowsuit and mittens, and strap him into his backpack.

Standing at our rough boat landing, I had to time my leap into the skiff at just the right moment. We'd launch ourselves off the rocks: me perched on the stern of the skiff with a baby on my back, while Thomas rowed us across the harbor, dodging the heaving lobster boats and mooring stumps. My baby surveyed these proceedings as if they were completely normal, often sleeping the whole way across.

The islanders looked askance at us, but Thomas's bravado kept them at a distance. Mostly they were kind to me, though I'm sure they thought I was mentally deficient. Actually, I was mainly trying like hell to be the person that Thomas expected me to be.

Early on, I did make attempts to demonstrate some independence, but there simply was not enough room for me to stand out in our life together. Most of my emotional time in our relationship was taken up attempting to be someone else's female ideal. I quickly learned to keep my mouth shut and fade into the woodwork.

In those days there was a restaurant in Waterville, Maine, called the Silent Woman. Its billboards were up and down I-95, depicting a headless lady serving dinner. That is who I became: The Silent Woman.

FLAT ASS CALM

CHAPTER THREE ~ MONHEGAN

You won't know why, and you can't say how
Such a change upon you came
But once you have slept on an island
You'll never be the same.

—*Rachel Field*

It should be noted that Thomas wasn't my first love. That honor belongs to a small pimple of land set miles out to sea, only six hundred acres large. Its lonely silhouette marks the easternmost boundary of the large, open Muscongus Bay. When viewed from the north or south, the shape of Monhegan's hunched profile, high on one end and tapering at the other, looks like nothing more than a huge whale's back, with tiny Manana as its tail. In 1569, the English explorer Thomas Ingram described it as:

> *...a great island that was backed like a whale. I first took it for a whale, as those fish in that country are easily taken for islands at a distance.*

Monhegan presently hosts a community of about 100 year-round souls. The population fluctuated during my years there from over 120, down to about seventy. Islands are not easy places to live, and

Monhegan, with its conflicting combination of congestion and isolation, was particularly difficult.

The village perches on the west side of the island, facing the small harbor formed by Manana on the west, a tiny islet called Smutty Nose to the north, and the wide-open Gulf of Maine to the south. Its houses are mostly weathered gray cedar shingled with white trim, clustered together in almost claustrophobic immediacy around a big central meadow.

The Meadow, round and crater-like, where whitetail deer grazed every evening, is the source of seasonal water for the town. The rhythmic thrum of the pumps can be heard during the summer months, sucking the water from the well points, up into storage tanks at the top of Lighthouse Hill. From there it would gravity feed to all the homes.

Monhegan village, with its jumble of houses, inns, shacks, and piled lobster traps, is overlooked by Lighthouse Hill, where the granite lighthouse stands, sending its warning beam out across the sea.

There are ancient fish houses grouped around Fish Beach, pickled into a state of seeming immortality by the literal tons of salt they hold to preserve the small herring baitfish that are stored within.

One small dirt road runs its short distance north to south from one end of the village to the other, with an arm extending over Horn's Hill toward the east, pointing toward a cliff called Burnt Head. There are no cars, just a few ancient trucks to service the store, inns, and lobster fishermen, as well as some golf carts.

It is an island of indescribable physical beauty—preserved in its natural state. Trails crisscross the majority of the island's 600 acres, over rocks, through damp forests and meadows, emerging at the top of towering cliffs with names like Blackhead and Whitehead ('head' being the old name for a headland or cliff) on the "backside" facing east. One path circumnavigates the island, following a torturous route starting at jumbled, rocky Pebble Beach to the north, then over headlands, diving down into crevasses, skirting huge rocks to end up at the far southern end of the island.

At the south end is Lobster Cove, where the old wreck of the *D.T. Sheridan* still lies like a rusty beached whale on the rocks above high tide. The *D.T. Sheridan*, a large tugboat hauling barges, went aground in 1948 on a flat calm day in pea-soup fog. The barges were saved, and no hands were lost. Many of the contents of that old tugboat can still be found decorating the island cottages: the ship's wheel hanging on a wall, or the giant bollards used to secure the massive ropes for towing living out their days as a bench in a yard.

Wreck of the D.T. Sheridan at Lobster Cove (Bob McMullen)

Monhegan is famous for its shipwrecks, being the most shipwrecked area on the coast of Maine. Local legend describes how on one stormy night, only a few years before I arrived, a young couple lost their lives when their sailboat went aground off Lobster Cove. The boat was discovered high aground the next morning, with the drowned woman lashed to the mast and her dead husband washed up on the nearby shore. The lead keel is all that remains, wedged between rocks, endlessly caressed by the tides.

As children, we were constantly warned never to go near the water on the eastern side, or 'backside' of the island. There, the combers—huge unpredictable waves—would snatch you away, your living, breathing visage never to be seen again. Many gruesome and true tales backed up these warnings, with the most notable being the tragic story of Jackie and Edward.

Back in the 1920s, when a group of teenagers were climbing on the rocks at the base of Whitehead, young Edward saw his friend Jackie slip and fall into the sea. He heroically dove in to save her, but both of them drowned; today, the little island library is dedicated to their memory. Coincidentally, Edward was also the older brother of my mother's first husband.

Jackie and Edward's Library book plate (Ellen Vaughan collection)

I connect to Monhegan through family. My mother's first marriage in the early 1940s was to a young man named Bill Vaughan. Bill's family was descended from Boston Brahmins and he was likely considered an enormous catch for a girl from the other side of the tracks in Southbridge, Massachusetts. Unfortunately, my poor mother had no idea what she was getting herself into.

Bill's mother was descended from the Cabots, the very same Cabots for which this old toast was coined:

And this is good old Boston,

the home of the bean and the cod.

Where Lowells speak only to Cabots,

and Cabots speak only to God.

Whether she actually spoke to God or not, Mrs. Vaughan was a thoroughly unpleasant mother-in-law to her son's new bride, Dora. The women and children of that family, along with their servants, would descend upon Monhegan every summer to take up residence in their summerhouse, while the men stayed in the city to work. Once the steamer trunks were unpacked and the cook was ensconced in the kitchen, these genteel Bostonians spent their summers lording it over the simple island folk in a refined and predictable fashion. It took almost no time at all for my mother to realize she was way out of her depth.

The Vaughan House (Ellen Vaughan)

The Vaughan family summers on Monhegan during the forties revolved around following the rules. There were rules regarding when mealtimes would happen and what would be served; when bridge parties would take place and who would attend; what could be worn and when, and so forth. My mother hated it with a deep purple passion and longed for her freedom. She finally convinced her husband to summer inshore in the coastal town of Friendship, away from her controlling mother-in-law. But by then, like generations of Vaughans before them, her children had already lost their hearts to Monhegan.

In the early seventies, Bill Vaughan gifted his family summer home to his grown children, my half-siblings Will, Ellen, and Frank. The "Vaughan House," a lovely antique Cape Cod House built around 1850, still sits placidly on the edge of the Meadow in the center of the village. Starting when I was three, I would spend some of my summers in this home and it soon became entwined with my love for the island.

Across the main dirt road from the Vaughan House is Swim Beach, a small strip of sand and rocks, where summering mothers took their children to swim, exchange gossip, and tan their bodies in the sun like oiled seals.

Nearby is Fish Beach, with its fish houses where the daily catch was cleaned. During my childhood, Fish Beach was a graveyard of fish in various stages of decay. They started out as fresh mutilated carcasses of cod, hake, haddock, and cusk, then were stripped of their fillets, tongues, and cheeks (by the fishermen), and eyeballs (by the gulls). Soon the fish became mere skeletons: sharp spiky bones barely held together by cartilage and skin, skulls gleaming whitely, all drifting lazily in the incoming tide. Later, when all the cod were fished out, the beach cleaned up considerably. Today it's still the place where the lobstermen pull up their skiffs after a long day at sea. The fish houses now host small seafood restaurants in the summer, and serve as bait storage in the winter.

On an overturned soapbox in front of the Vaughan House, my sister Irene and I sold ashtrays and soap dishes to the tourists, which were sea clam shells we had brought up from Cape Cod for that purpose. The minute we sold something we would run to the nearby Island Spa gift shop to blow our earnings on penny candy and cheap wind-up toys.

Our brother Frank was a tall and awkward teenager with a keen business sense. Very early on, he became an entrepreneur with an actual store set up near Swim Beach to sell his wares. His store was an old rotted dory, propped up against lobster traps. There he and his best friend Lexi sold cured starfish, sea urchins, and sand dollars that they gleaned from tide pools, and small wooden buoys they had carved by hand and painted. The Vaughan House was often redolent with the smells of boiling starfish and drying sea urchins.

Hand Carved Lobster Buoys by Frank and Lexi (Ellen Vaughan collection)

Frank also fixed up old skiffs to take tourists to Manana; I worked for him when I was in my early teens, rowing people across the harbor for seventy-five cents a trip. His sign, posted out in front of the Vaughan House, proclaimed:

Manana Tours!

See the Hermit!

The Viking Inscriptions!

The Coast Guard Station!

And

The Bottomless Pool!

Frank would take groups of people out in his old motorboat to see the harbor seals; fat, sausage-shaped creatures with big liquid eyes that would pull themselves up on nearby tiny rock islands at low tide. Frank would interrupt his seal tour by stopping partway out with his boatload of tourists to gather his fares, figuring that collecting while surrounded by water would guarantee payment.

George Bellows (1882-1925) "Cleaning Fish" 1913

Frank thought Irene and I were the worst pests, but sometimes he managed to put up with us tagging along with him as he went about his various moneymaking endeavors. On one memorable fishing trip, we caught a pregnant dogfish. Dogfish are small sharks with a sharp spine on their backs; they bear their young live. Frank slit the belly of the fish and out popped five baby sharks, their embryonic sacks still attached. He put them in a bucket of water and brought them home, later transferring them to old glass battery containers we found in the shed, which served as small aquariums until we took pity and let the doomed creatures go.

Monhegan was a place of complete magic for a child. The olfactory memories of it are still firmly implanted in my mind: the smell of iron sewer pipes belching their toilet-papery contents onto the rocks at low tide, and an overpowering stench of salted herring—gone just slightly bad in the fish houses. There was the oily reek of kerosene lamps glowing softly against the many-paned windows of an antique cape cottage, the hint of propane exhaust from a generator putt-putting away in its shed, the tantalizingly sweet perfume of the scarlet rugosa rose blossoms, or best of all, the heady scent of the balsam fir in the spookily silent woods, carpeted thickly with needles, moss, and ferns, and cut with slanting rays of sunlight. It was a pungent combination of rot, decay, and fecund renewal that pervaded that tiny island with an everlasting stink.

Fish Beach (Penobscot Marine Museum)

Monhegan was a place of wonderment where sneaky adults would build fairy houses from sticks, moss, and pebbles to charm the children. We kids would climb the towering dangerous rock cliffs on the headlands like monkeys. We had a blast out there as only children can. We climbed every precipice, rowed skiffs around the harbor, caught mackerel and baby pollock off the dock, and went deep-sea fishing for cod, huge ugly fish as big as we were. We took apart and re-assembled fish skeletons we found on Fish Beach, stringing the vertebrae along with periwinkle shells on necklaces, and dressed up in my siblings' long-dead grandmother's clothes, boldly parading around town in dated old lady dresses, gaily waving delicate parasols.

It was a natural heaven for me, a child already entranced by nature. But even more than that, the island was family. The villagers were friendly, but brooked no nonsense from us kids. We would get yelled at if we threw gravel off the wharf or were found climbing on stacked lobster traps. They let us ride around the island on their truck tailgates, showed us how to gut fish, always said hello on the road, and shared their fascinating rites of work and life with us. We heard stories of life and death: the fisherman who fell off his boat in the harbor with his boots on and was found standing upright underwater just a stone's throw from the beach, or the search for the man who disappeared in the woods and wasn't found until the following spring, sitting against a tree as dried up as a stick.

"Backside" of Monhegan

When I was ten I spent a whole day with an old lobsterman named Henley Day who was digging a grave in the cemetery. He told me his views of life and politics, which flew way over my head, while he carefully scraped out a perfect rectangle of a hole exactly six feet deep.

We would watch buoys being painted, lobster traps repaired, boats overhauled, pot warp coiled, all the while being instructed as to what we were seeing and how it all fit into the scheme of life.

This wondrous existence struck a chord within me so strongly that I grew up obsessed with the place and constantly ached to be there. My home at the time was on Cape Cod, where my parents had an art gallery in the town of Wellfleet. They were more than happy to send us away to get us out from underfoot, so they'd pack me and my sister off to Monhegan under the care of an older sister or brother to spend the summer.

Some summers we remained on the Cape, where I still had fun playing with the fiddler crabs in the salt marshes, swimming in the warm bay, or digging up cherrystone clams with my toes. Although not Monhegan, it was a lovely life... until it all went to shit.

Old Monhegan Postcard

By the time I was ten, I had a recurring dream of boarding the mail boat to return to the island. We'd arrive and everyone on the wharf was waving and wildly happy to see me. I would walk up Wharf Hill toward my siblings' house, so suffused with incredible joy that I was almost crying. Then I would wake up to find myself back wherever I happened to be. This dream happened over and over again, and it left no doubt in my mind that the only antidote would be a permanent retreat back to the first love of my life, Monhegan Island.

FLAT ASS CALM

CHAPTER FOUR ~ TEENAGE CRUSH

The heart has its reasons, which reason knows not of.

—Pascal

I first met Thomas when I was a young teen summering on Monhegan in 1973. I was fascinated by the mysterious, long-haired young man wearing a black cape and dark glasses, striding barefoot down the road. His fingernails and toenails were painted black and he was accompanied by a nanny goat on a leash. He had thick, honey-blond hair to his shoulders, a bearded face, and was obviously much older than I.

Being only fourteen and too shy to approach, I watched him covertly as groups of us waited outside the store for its evening opening. Two brothers, Doug and Harry Odom, ran the island's only store. They were both in their fifties, confirmed bachelors, and big-time alcoholics.

When they finally showed up to open the store, they were invariably drunk. Sometimes they didn't make it at all, having passed out at their sister's house where they always took their supper. These two brothers would later give me my first job: running the cash register and meeting the mail boat in their dilapidated truck to haul groceries up to the store to be put away.

Meeting the boat was, and still is, the major social event on the island. Monhegan has only one wharf and it juts out into the narrow gut, or passage, between the main island and the tiny island, Smutty Nose. The wharf is built of large granite blocks weighing many tons. Hewn from a mainland quarry, these blocks were transported by barge and stacked in a crazed geometric asymmetry to form a solid imposing peninsula.

Monhegan wharf at boat time (Bob McMullen)

If you climb down the ladders that grip the vertical sides of the wharf, you will find starfish, mussels, and pink sea anemones tucked into the granite seams at low tide, along with a mesmerizing suck and blow of endless flows of seawater around the nooks and crannies. As a child I would spend a lot of time looking over the side of the wharf into the clear water, trying to identify the trash that lay strewn on the bottom. In those days everyone simply threw their garbage off the wharf, though efforts were underway to have a lobster boat haul the stuff out a mile or two and then throw it overboard. I could see old lawn chairs, crockery, paint cans, magazines, and roofing shingles all jumbled together to form a harbor bottom of riotous complexity. Along with seeking shells on the island's beaches, we looked for sea glass, old chains rusted into tortured shapes, the pencil-thick black cores of flashlight batteries—smooth as lozenges—or a piece of pottery, worn to worry-stone softness, showing a tiny glimpse of its pattern. It was here that I learned how trash could become treasure.

The slip was a heavy wooden ramp on the wharf. It could be raised and lowered by pulling a chain that turned a wheel that was attached to gears, pulleys, and more chains. This allowed people to disembark from boats no matter how low the tide. Raising and lowering the slip and catching the lines from the mail boat as she slid alongside the wharf were considered jobs of immense importance to us children. Meeting the boat was a responsibility we took seriously, and it was with a sense of great duty that we helped unload the boxes, crates, mail sacks, luggage, and the occasional large appliance at boat time.

Who was coming and going from the island was duly noted, as well as what and who they were bringing with them. The constant undercurrent of murmurings went something like this:

"Ah, I see that Bob has a new color TV; hmmm he must be doing well to afford that."

"And what's that? *Another* generator for the school? What's wrong with the old one?"

"Well! Isn't this the *third* time Joanie's been inshore this month? What's up with *her*?"

It was all a marvelous muddle of activity and gossip that we eagerly awaited every day.

It was during the bustle of boat time that I found the courage to approach the mysterious young Thomas and strike up a conversation. It was a casual encounter, but I was intrigued. I had made some friends that summer, mostly young people who would share their weed with me and some older people who would buy beer for us. But this guy was something different.

The large inn at the top of the hill employed a number of college-age kids, and their dorms were places to hang out and get wasted. I didn't have access to Thomas's circle of friends, so I had to make do with young men who didn't interest me, all of whom tried unsuccessfully to get me to sleep with them. I was still a virgin and terrified of sex, but being a free spirit from California at the time, I

33

thought nothing of wearing short shorts and filmy shirts with no bra. I was painfully young and unaware, still a child uncomfortably ensconced in the body of a woman. On an island full of sexually liberated, testosterone-charged young men, I could have been easy prey, but though they tried to coerce me, they wouldn't force me. Or perhaps I was just lucky enough to not be in the wrong place at the wrong time with the wrong man.

Steamer Landing at Monhegan Island, ME (Penobscot Marine Museum)

The night before I left the island that summer, I was invited to a party at Thomas's house. He was staying in a tiny shed behind his parents' summer cottage and would frequently throw large parties; the little shack would rock on its foundations to the thumping chords of the Rolling Stones and Jimi Hendrix, it was constantly engulfed with billowing clouds of marijuana smoke, and usually packed with stoned bodies. I had been *dying* to be invited.

Unfortunately, that night, we all got high so quickly that we passed out before the night was half over. Just before I lost consciousness, sprawling out on the floor, Thomas reached over, took my hand in his, and gazed into my eyes. That was all that happened that night between us. I left the next day not to return for two years, but I felt the impression of his hand in mine all the while.

When I returned to California that fall, my recurring dreams of Monhegan started up once again, only now they also featured the eyes of a mysterious young man.

FLAT ASS CALM

PART II

FLAT ASS CALM

CHAPTER FIVE ~ CAPE COD

The web of our life is of a mingled yarn, good and ill together.

—*Shakespeare*

As a child, I was the quintessential tomboy. I had reached the conclusion, somewhere around age six, that someone had made a grave mistake with my gender selection. I knew that I was supposed to be a boy; the fact that I was a lousy girl was a never-ending source of disappointment. I would look at my smooth body after my bath, trying with all my might to make a penis magically appear. This desire for a different gender didn't last long and by the time I reached puberty it had completely disappeared. My unwillingness to conform to feminine norms, however, has remained with me.

No penis forthcoming, I had to compensate by being boyish in every other way I could. I wore boy's clothes, climbed trees, and threw rocks. I played endlessly with bugs, toads, snakes, and small animals, dead or alive.

Many of my childhood hours were spent exploring the Cape Cod salt marshes in Wellfleet and Truro, keeping company with fiddler crabs and periwinkle snails. Once I found an abandoned rowboat and paddled it around the marsh for days, until the tide finally reclaimed it. I figured out how to catch the minnows that were living in the stream behind our house and brought a bucket of them home. My mother came in the kitchen to find me boiling a huge pot of small dead fish on the stove for the cat. The smell was memorable.

Cape Cod tomboy, ca. mid-1960s

The day that I caught a black racer was one of my biggest thrills. Black racers are beautiful, sleek, non-venomous snakes three to four feet long. They are very fast, and I had to learn to move quickly to catch one. I found the best method was to step on the snake's body just hard enough to pin it down. Then as he swung his head back and bit my pants leg, I would grab him just behind the head, quick as lightning. My idea of a great joke one day was to wrap the snake around my neck a couple of times and ring the front doorbell to our house. My poor mother never fully recovered from that one.

I was a very shy, introverted tomboy, and had a hard time making friends. The more I changed schools, the harder it got for me.

Any human friendship was a serious affair for me and I clung to the relationship like a limpet.

The constant disruptions in our home contributed to my introversion. I gravitated toward the woods, marsh, and my love of nature as my sanctuary. Books provided a much-needed refuge as well, and I mostly read adventure novels (Hardy boys, *never* Nancy Drew) and books on nature. Some well-meaning family member gave me a guide to owning a wild animal for a pet and, as a result, I pestered my parents endlessly for a skunk. I had to settle for a gerbil.

My parents put up with my antics with the tolerance born of having many children grown and gone from the nest. I was the last of eight children; each of my parents had left behind a former spouse and three kids in order to be together, which in the 1950s, was scandalous behavior indeed.

Al on Monhegan

My father, Alfred (called Al by all who knew him), was a handsome man who bore more than a faint resemblance to Cary Grant. Born in 1920, he was descended on his father's side from German immigrants who settled near Rochester, New York, in the mid-nineteenth century. His mother's forebears were German and English, and they had settled in Virginia during the seventeenth and nineteenth centuries. Al grew up in Wayland, New York, and studied art at Syracuse University. He became a graphics designer for Kodak, and went on to teach art at the University of Rochester.

Al's father, Alfred Sr., was a stern, unpleasant man who had started out by singing in penny operas during the first two decades of the 1900s. Then, in his thirties, he decided to settle down, obtain an accounting degree, and get married. My paternal grandfather can only be described as an insufferably sanctimonious and disagreeable jerk; he was thoroughly disliked by pretty much every member of the family.

His wife, Grace Greenwood, who died long before I was born, had a family history worth noting. She was descended from the earliest British settlers in Virginia, as well as German burghers who came over in the early nineteenth century. Both sides of her family were slaveholders and two of her great-grandfathers fought for the Confederacy.

Grace's German immigrant great-uncle, a soap maker named William Greenwood, did split dramatically from his slaveholding family when he took Martha Sparrow, a free woman of color, as his "wife" in the early 1800s (marriage was illegal between different races at that time). Apparently, the rest of the Greenwoods disapproved so strongly of the union that they did not include William or his family to join their 1855 flight from a Norfolk yellow fever epidemic. William died in that epidemic, leaving his common-law wife and their five children to fend for themselves.

William and Martha's third great-grandson, Rev. C. Bernard Ruffin III, contacted my father and uncle out of the blue many years ago, after he'd completed detailed genealogical research on his family that led him to our door. His book, *Kemp, Sparrow and Greenwood Families of Norfolk, Virginia* is a great account of his family's place in Virginia history before, during, and after the Civil War. He traces the lives of white slaveholders, the enslaved women they took to bed, and their offspring, as well as my outlier great-uncle, his consort, and their children. I remember how amused my father and his brother were when they learned their family had an African-American branch, because they knew their much-disliked and fortunately dead father would have hated it beyond reason. It turned out that the Greenwoods had skeletons in their closets that they simply never talked about.

My father married his first wife in the early 1940s and they had two children, Eric and Helga. They lived on a small farm in Springwater, New York, where he grew Christmas trees in his spare time.

My mother, Dora was born in 1922 and came from French-Canadian, Irish, and English immigrants who settled around Southbridge, Massachusetts, to work in the mills during the Industrial Revolution. She was a beautiful woman, short and slender, with wavy dark hair, a great sense of humor, and a sharp wit.

Dora didn't speak of her family much. She claimed that she has no use for any of them. She especially disliked her mother, a diminutive woman with a strong French-Canadian accent who grew huge gardens and was described by Dora as the original health food freak. My mother would often relate, with almost palpable outrage, how she was never allowed to have popcorn at the movies. Instead her mother would send off to the show with a dime for admission and a head of lettuce to munch on. This apparently scarred my mother for life.

Dora's father was an alcoholic who died of cirrhosis before I was born. He was set off to work in the knife factory when he was little more than a child to help support his widowed mother, until she died in the flu pandemic around 1919 and he was finally able to seek a wife of his own. He had one sister named Mary, and Dora recalled that her Aunt Mary longed to own one of the bungalow-style homes that were all the rage back in the 1920s and 30s, often telling Dora that someday she would have her very own little "boogaloo."

Unfortunately, Mary suffered a psychotic break when she was in her thirties. When her dysfunction became apparent and she could no longer work, she moved in with Dora's family, until she attacked Dora's mother with a teaspoon and was sent to live out her days in a mental institution.

My mother collected stories. She would retell family legends—some humorous, some not so much—over and over again, often with a big belly laugh. She also wiped her mind clean of the things that were uncomfortable or unpleasant to her. It was a quirk, I guess.

Aunt Mary

I've tried many times to define my mother, but always find it difficult, as she was definitely one of a kind. One of the most important things she valued was good taste. Everything she looked at in the world was judged and categorized into one of two groups: good taste or bad taste. An original and interesting ceramic fountain was good taste. A glass globe garden ornament was bad taste. Most peoples' homes were decorated in very bad taste, according to my mother. She hated mass-produced art, tacky kitsch, and things with ruffles. My mother's most withering insult was, "All their taste is in their mouth." I have no idea where she picked up these ideas of aesthetics, but they remained a fixation for her entire adult life.

After my mother's death in 2010, I dug out all of her old photo albums—long stored away but somehow safeguarded through many moves—to try to get a fresh look at this woman who'd had such an enormous influence over my life.

Sepia-toned photos of Dora as an infant in the early 1920s, Dora dressed up as a scowling ballerina, or in various outfits posing in photographic studios. Dora canoeing on Webster Lake, which she insisted on calling by its original Indian name: Lake Chargoggagoggmanchauggagoggchaubunagungamaugg, which apocryphally translates to, "You fish on your side, I'll fish on my side, and nobody fish in the middle". As the photos progress in time, they show her transitioning from adolescence into a lovely young woman, with slim hips and an impish smile. There are many, many pictures that obviously were taken with care, even love.

Dora on Webster Lake

It was difficult to reconcile these images with the stories I had been told of a childhood devoid of any warmth, where Dora's father preferred the barroom to his home, and her mother's smoldering resentments and controlling nature fueled her need to dictate every aspect of her daughter's life.

I remembered Dora telling me that her mother picked out all of her friends, and made sure every one of them was less attractive than she, so she would shine the brightest. And how as a very small child she was dispatched by her mother to the local bar down the street to beg her father to come home for dinner. And how her father never touched her, either in love nor anger.

And yet these photos of a serene young woman paddling the canoe with her beloved cocker spaniel on a lake with an unpronounceable name don't support these stories. Nor do all the shots of her standing next to girlfriends indicate that they are ugly ducklings next to Dora's swan-like beauty. They all looked like average happy young women of their time.

Sometimes a picture can tell you a thousand words, while other times it doesn't tell you a damned thing.

After she graduated from high school, my mother attended music school (she was a piano player). She then studied to become a secretary before she married her first husband, Bill Vaughan, in 1942. They settled in Massachusetts and had three children, Will, Ellen, and Frank. In the mid-1950s, Bill's job required them to move their family to Rochester, New York, which turned out to be fateful indeed.

***

My oldest sister, Ellen, would often relate a story about how, soon after they moved to Rochester, our mother signed her up for art classes at the local university. Ellen would come home after class and gush about her *very* handsome art teacher. The next thing Ellen remembers is her mother announcing to her and her brothers that she was divorcing their father and marrying the art teacher. Ellen definitely didn't see that coming.

My father's former wife and kids were moved off the Springwater farm and my mother and her three kids moved in. Al's first wife was eight months pregnant with my half-sister Celia when she was dispatched to Juarez, Mexico, for their divorce, while my mother, now three months pregnant with my sister Irene, waited in the wings to marry Al. It was a pretty muddled time, to put it mildly.

46

Al teaching art in Rochester, NY. Ca. mid-1950s

After I was born in 1959, my parents hatched a scheme to leave the farm in Springwater, along with all the drama they'd created, and start over someplace new. Al would quit his teaching job to live out his dream as a full-time contemporary artist, and together they would open a gallery. My father's paintings and sculpture at that time were largely expressionistic, with occasional forays into more abstract forms. He was a skilled craftsman and a prodigious producer of artwork. The man lived to paint and sculpt.

My parents departed New York and moved to Wellfleet, Massachusetts around 1960. There they started one of the first contemporary art galleries on outer Cape Cod, helping to launch Wellfleet as the art community it is today

While we maintained a close relationship, with my mother's three earlier children and even her ex-husband, we completely lost contact with my father's kids after we left New York. He simply walked away from his old life and if he maintained any connection with any of them, I was not aware of it. I don't believe my half-sister Celia even met her father until she was sixteen years old. Al's former wife supported herself and her children by working as a teacher. How they made it financially is a mystery to me because to my knowledge, they never received any child support. We were so cut off that I never met my paternal half-siblings until I was in my early twenties, when Eric sought me out, and I was thirty-eight years old before I finally met my long-lost sister, Celia.

I can't say I understand my father's frame of mind when he committed this abandonment of his children, but there is little doubt that it had many lasting repercussions on their lives. I think they all mostly forgave him later in life, but I don't believe he ever admitted, nor took ownership of, his massive shortcomings in the fatherhood department to them, or to any of us for that matter. In fact, neither of my parents were good at acknowledging their fuckups.

My parents' gallery in Wellfleet was started in the old house they bought perched on the edge of a small pond near Route 6. Over time, the gallery grew to represent over twenty artists as it slowly expanded into a large converted garage out back, with added sculpture gardens and small ornamental pools, complete with tasteful burbling ceramic water fountains.

Wellfleet gallery sculpture garden

Growing up in an art gallery wasn't easy; three words I heard continually throughout my young childhood were, "Don't touch that!"

My sister and I were two little kids surrounded by fragile objects, and we had to keep our hands to ourselves.

Irene is two years my senior and we were a study in opposites. Her dark brown hair, brown eyes, and olive skin was a direct contrast to my blonde hair, blue eyes, and fair, freckled skin. I was convinced that Irene lived to tease and torment me. We shared a bed when we were little and had vigorous wrestling matches, which I always lost. We played endless "touched you last" games (I always lost). She could run faster, shout louder, pinch harder, make incredibly smelly farts, and generally torture me in hundreds of ways. She was a typical older sister.

Our father was a stern disciplinarian and Irene, more than I, bore the brunt of his rages. The belt was his favorite tool to mete out punishment, and I feared it more than anything. Irene was a defiant child, and she suffered from our father's belt far too often. These spankings seemed to produce the opposite of their desired effect, and Irene's acting out became more dedicated and frequent as she grew older.

As with our looks, Irene and I also had contrasting personalities, so against the turbulent backdrop of Irene's naughtiness, I assumed the role of the compliant child who never enjoyed conflict and who always tried to bring peace to our often-troubled home. Not to say that I wasn't naughty too, but I was a lot sneakier about it.

When I was about nine, a new girl moved into town. Her name was Kate and her father was another artist. They had a new gallery in South Wellfleet. I'm afraid my father didn't think much of Kate's father's paintings; they were flamboyant affairs depicting obese horses with pronounced genitalia galloping wildly around in large herds.

Kate was spoiled and totally unfaithful—sometimes my best friend, other times ganging up on me with other mean girls—but we did manage to get into trouble together. One of our favorite kicks during the off-season was climbing onto the roofs of (we hoped) unoccupied summer homes. We would search out unlocked windows, crawl in, and explore inside the empty cottages. It was mostly a matter of rummaging through the drawers and pantries with the terror of being discovered accompanying every furtive footstep.

When Kate came to stay with me in town, we would walk the streets of Wellfleet searching for cigarette butts to smoke. We'd swagger around feeling very grown up—two nine-year-olds puffing away on someone's discarded, broken, lipstick-stained Marlboro (fortunately this was as far as I ever got at cigarette smoking).

We swiped candy bars from Lema's Market and I vividly remember the first wonderful bite of a stolen Mounds Bar. Unfortunately, Kate got nabbed later when she tried to lift another candy bar by herself. Her description of having to go to the police station put me off thievery for quite some time. I had a huge horror of being caught.

We spent a lot of time riding my new bicycle around town. It was a really cool bike, with a banana seat and spider handlebars. We would both fit comfortably on the big seat, sharing the pedals together. In this fashion we could be seen, racing madly around the narrow streets of Wellfleet, with cars going by close enough to touch.

Kate wasn't my first real friend. A few years before my parents separated, they bought a second home a few miles away, in Truro. This was to be our home away from the gallery, which had grown to take over almost every room in the Wellfleet house. Irene and I constantly had to give up our bedrooms to accommodate more wall space for paintings, and floor space for sculpture pedestals. I suspect that at times, my parents considered the attic as a possible storage place for their offspring.

When we went to look at the new house, we passed a ramshackle cottage, located at the bottom of our prospective abode's steep driveway, with a yard covered with discarded toys and rubbish. My parents groaned, very unhappy to find that there was obviously some sort of trashy people living right next door. Despite this blot on the landscape, they bought the Truro house.

Our new neighbors turned out to be a woman with six children, ranging from four years old to late teens. Cathy, one of the daughters, was my age and another daughter was Irene's age. Cathy was a little waif with big eyes, long wavy hair, and a certain toughness that I admired. We immediately became fast friends, spending every possible moment together. My only regret was that I still had to go back to

Wellfleet to go to school (my parents claimed the school in Truro was, well... trashy).

Truro House

For me, a trip to Cathy's house was like an adventure to a third world country. Our home was always excruciatingly neat and clean. My most vivid memories of my father are him bending over to pick a piece of lint off the carpet. He simply couldn't bear to have any disorder in his life. He tidied, cleaned, and scrubbed up after us, and constantly harangued us to clean our rooms. If I came home to use the bathroom and left my bicycle by the door, invariably I would find the bike put away in the garage when I came back. When my mother put down the newspaper and went for a cup of coffee, the newspaper would be neatly folded and put away by the time she returned. Our refrigerators always had the enamel worn off the fronts due to constant scouring with Comet Cleanser. Once my father tried experimenting with various cleaning agents and combined bleach and ammonia to disinfect the toilet. That was nearly his *last* cleaning chemistry experiment.

The first time I went to Cathy's house, I thought an explosion had taken place there. Clothes, toys, and trash were strewn about. There wasn't a clean dish in the house. The dog was up on the kitchen table licking the butter. The TV was on all the time, blaring daytime soaps. Kids were running around partially clothed, totally oblivious to the chaos around them. It smelled like dirty laundry and urine.

I thought it was *great*.

We went to Cathy's room where all her clothes were in a mound in a corner. Her bed was unmade, and clutter of enormous proportions was everywhere. We jumped up and down on her pee-soaked mattress and no one cared.

Our Truro house perched on a hill overlooking the Pamet River. The Pamet is a lazy, winding tidal stream, snaking through the salt marshes on its way to Cape Cod Bay. In the winter the river froze and heaved giant blocks of ice around with each tide. Once we ventured out onto the rotten salt ice at high tide and I fell through; fortunately, it was shallow enough that the water only came up to my chest. We slunk back to Cathy's house with my teeth chattering, trailing ice and salt water. We quickly dried my clothes there so that my parents would never find out.

Cathy's sister and Irene once got stranded on an ice floe and floated way up the river on an incoming tide. Someone in town saw them and firemen and police were dispatched to the rescue.

Summers on the Pamet were delightful. Cathy and I played in the river, poked the horseshoe crabs, and swam in the warm brown waters when the tide was in. At low tide I walked barefoot in the mud to feel for cherrystone clams with my toes. When I got a little older, I would open them with a knife and swallow their warm salty bodies raw.

The marsh was a maze of deep riverbed cuts and we slogged through the mud in all of them, playing hide-and-seek, or hunkering down now and then to admire or harass the myriad of creatures that lived there. We collected mussels from their nearby beds, bringing them home by the bucketful to be steamed open and eaten. Whole days were spent in the woods climbing trees and playing explorers. In the spring the box turtles came out of hibernation and we would hold tortoise races—a game requiring a *great* deal of patience.

Cape Cod Box Turtle

At one point our parents became alarmed at the amount of time Irene and I spent with these neighbor children. As soon as we arrived in Truro we'd be off like a shot down the hill and not seen again until they'd call, often until they were hoarse, for us to come home for supper. So they came up with a rule that we were not to play on Sundays; we could not leave the property and no friends could come over. We were all completely nonreligious, but for some reason our Sundays were held out as being a "day of rest" in the best old-timey Christian tradition.

We hated our Sundays off, so we moped around and were miserable. We tried to get around the restriction by calling down the hill and yelling back and forth at our friends. When this was discouraged, I came up with another scheme; there was a huge old willow tree in Cathy's yard that loomed higher than our yard up the hill. I instructed Cathy to climb this tree, so we could be at eye level and not have to shout very loudly at each other, and thus avoid detection. This worked well until Cathy fell out of the tree, breaking her clavicle. Shortly thereafter the tree was cut down. Eventually our parents tired of having us underfoot on Sundays, and released us to run free again.

View of high tide on the Pamet River

Cathy and I were always barefoot and shirtless on those warm summer days and I remember well our declaring wholeheartedly that we planned to stay kids forever. This was before my parent's divorce, and life was as good as it would ever get. I instinctively knew that I didn't want it to end.

Unfortunately, it came to a crashing halt on the day that my sister ridiculed me for going topless and showing my budding breasts to the world. In this harsh fashion, I was unwillingly pushed over the threshold of adolescence. Gone forever was that wonderful sense of being a child, of feeling totally at ease with my world and myself. I was shown a fig leaf and told to get the hell out of paradise.

It was around that time that I became aware that my parents were having long, disturbing "discussions" every evening. They would retire to the living room after dinner with their drinks, and the decibel level of their conversations would rise as the evening, and number of drinks, progressed. Irene and I would nervously stand in the doorway and ask them what they were arguing about, only be told firmly that these were not arguments, they were "discussions." Of course, later I realized that this was the beginning of the end of their marriage. They simply started to disagree about almost everything.

My parents' divorce in the late 1960s was a devastating rift in our family. My father left for another life and another woman, leaving my mother unable to cope with her second divorce and what she likely saw as the failure of her life. She immediately plunged into the bottle, dragging my sister and me under with her. Irene responded by acting out; I responded by turning within. Irene tore things apart and I tried to put them back together again. At the tender ages of ten and twelve, our lives as children of a divorce became a shameful secret. In our little rural backwater on the Cape, none of our friends had divorced parents. In those days, it simply wasn't talked about.

FLAT ASS CALM

CHAPTER SIX ~ DAMNED MEMORIES

The first half of our lives is ruined by our parents,
and the second half by our children.

—*Clarence Darrow*

I was born with a prodigious memory. This may be looked upon as a blessing or a curse; it's a blessing if you are trying to write a memoir, but it can be a curse because some of these memories would be better off long forgotten.

My first memory is of sitting with my sister, Irene, in the back seat of our car. Our parents were looking at the house they were buying in Wellfleet. I was about one and a half or two, so it must have been around 1961. My next vivid memory is probably about a year later. I was playing outside and noticed what I envisioned to be colorful little soldiers lined up in a row in the dirt along the foundation of the garage. I carefully broke off the little soldiers from their anchors in the ground and placed them in a neat pile... until my mother saw me. I guess the sight of her tow-headed child diligently picking every unopened tulip bud in the garden upset her because she immediately rushed out of the house and slapped me. I had no idea what I had done wrong.

The next notable event happened when I was about three. While taking my afternoon nap I had a vivid dream that I was able to fly down the stairs and soar around the house with complete abandon. I awoke, walked to the top of the stairs, spread my arms wide, and launched myself off. Instead of flying, I went thump, thump, thump down the stairs and landed in a heap at the bottom, knocked out cold. I was rushed to the hospital where I was diagnosed with a concussion.

My second concussion was when I was about four. Irene and I were riding tricycles in the front of the house in Wellfleet. We were riding Irene's big tricycle, tear-assing down the driveway when we hit a rock, tipped over and crashed to the ground, with me on the bottom (of course). The world went around and round and my face was a mass of embedded crushed oyster shells.

My parents have often told me that when I was quite small, I would periodically go into fugue states where I would stare into space with my mouth open for extended periods of time. Once I engaged in this strange activity while sitting in the back seat of our car as our family was driving somewhere. I guess they couldn't rouse me so, with great concern, my parents drove to the nearest doctor's office. Of course, I eventually came back to earth and the doc didn't have a clue what was wrong (he told them I was "tired") so he sent us on our way. I remember being woken out of these space adventures every once in a while. Eventually they went away.

Among my happiest early memories of the Cape were of us going to the beach. On Sundays in the summer the gallery was closed, so we would all pile into our 1957 Willys Jeep and head for Duck Harbor. My parents always drove the Jeep off-road to an area of the beach where no one else went. There we would picnic, swim, and hunt for shells, skate egg cases, and goose fish. It was in the warm waters of Cape Cod Bay that I learned to swim. I have since reached the conclusion that it was there that I got what amounted to a transfusion of seawater into my veins, linking me to the ocean for many decades of my life. I loved our beach days, and I was especially proud of my Tarzan bathing suit; a snazzy leopard-skin print affair with only one strap, leaving half of my chest bare.

At some point in my childhood, I figured out that our family was different. For one thing my father was an artist. None of my friends had fathers who were artists. I was also pretty sure that none of my friends had nude paintings of their mothers hanging on their walls. Dora would often model for Al, and they thought nothing of hanging her naked pictures all over the house and gallery. It did make for some awkward moments when my friends came over.

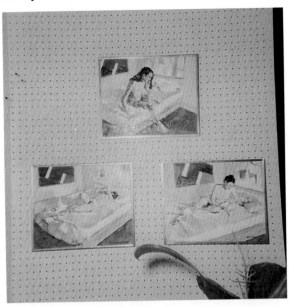

Nudes of my mother –Wellfleet Gallery

Another thing that set us apart was we never went to church. We didn't just not go to church, we were unaffiliated with any known religion. Whenever I tried to make friends at a new school, one of the first questions—as part of the inevitable dog butt-sniffing process of integration—was, "What church do *you* go to?" I always had to shrug my shoulders and say we didn't go to church, an answer that was invariably greeted with great incredulity. My early grade school years were also the last years of mandatory prayer in public schools, so every morning in class I would sit there uncomfortably trying to mimic my classmates, with their clasped hands and earnest praying faces, all the while wondering what the hell I was supposed to be doing.

Once I asked my mother in a very pained way, why couldn't we be like other kids and have a church too? She airily instructed me to tell my friends that we were "free spirits." So, I did. This information produced some puzzled looks, but it stopped the questions. Later my mother ran into one of the parents of my school friends at the grocery store. This lady informed Dora that she'd heard that the Free Spirits

Church held meetings at a certain downtown location if she'd like to attend. This amused Dora to no end.

Me on Cape Cod—early 1960s

Another thing that made us different was we moved around a lot. My parents soon found that a gallery on Cape Cod was deader than a doornail in the winter. Their solution to this seasonal lack of income was to pack up some choice pieces of art and seek places to relocate during the off-season. Once a suitable place was scouted out, they would open a little temporary gallery there.

We did this about every other year. So I spent kindergarten in New Hope, Pennsylvania, first grade in Wellfleet, second grade in Litchfield, Connecticut, third grade back in Wellfleet, until my disastrous fourth grade year when Dora took Irene and me to Sarasota, Florida, leaving my father home alone. This was the second winter they had gone separately to a winter location; the previous winter Al had gone to Delaware by himself to open a small gallery while we stayed on the Cape.

I suppose that the reasoning for my father going off alone that year was that all this moving around wasn't good for us kids—which was true. Unbeknownst to us however, things started happening in

Delaware with my father and another woman, something we didn't find out about until a year later.

The winter I was in fourth grade, Dora took Irene and me to Florida to open a gallery, while Al stayed home to paint. It was in Florida where my world was irrevocably turned upside down. We were renting a small house with big cockroaches on one of the Sarasota Keys, and I was having a really difficult time in school, having found myself at the very bottom of the pecking order and disliked by everyone in my class. I was naturally shy and the fact that I was a loathed Yankee in the south didn't help. It was an all-white segregated school and I'd never met a meaner bunch of kids.

Another big problem was that I was behind on memorizing my multiplication tables because the Wellfleet curriculum hadn't covered it yet. Math became a torture for me, and to this very day I still can't remember what eight times seven is. My fourth-grade Sarasota teacher was an unsympathetic woman who took great pleasure in ridiculing me for not being able to keep up. Following their teacher's lead, the rest of the students figured it was open season and never missed an opportunity to pick on me.

One little girl in our class (who I thought bore an incredible likeliness to the comedian Pat Paulson) actually swaggered up to me one morning and said, "I don't like you and I want to fight." She came up to my chin. I laughed at the idea, but she was dead serious. She told everyone that we were going to fight at recess and I immediately became terrified. I didn't know how to fight, and the idea of getting hurt turned my guts to jelly. Recess came, and I faced her, this tiny apparition dancing around me with her fists up. My mind went blank and the only thing I could think of to do was run away, followed closely by the jeers of all those who had gathered to watch.

I frequently came home from that school in tears. I once made up a story to tell my mother about how a boy picked on me, so I punched him in the nose. Dora told me that smacking that kid was the right thing to do and she heartily congratulated me. But the story wasn't true, and I didn't feel especially great about taking the credit for what was pretty sketchy advice from a parent to begin with.

One day I came home from school to find my mother sitting at the kitchen table with an opened letter and a bottle of beer in front of her. The table was littered with beer bottles and full ashtrays and she was crying. I asked what was wrong and she told me that Daddy had written a letter saying he wanted a divorce. I didn't even know what that meant. I asked why she was drinking a beer in the middle of the afternoon—I had never even seen her drink beer before. Dora said that she needed it to help stop the pain. Obviously, the pain was great, because beer and wine became her constant companions.

The rest of Florida was a blur of my mother crying and drinking all the time, my father coming down to help us drive home to the Cape, my mother crying all the way home with us kids bewildered and scared in the back seat, and me being relieved to be out of that horrible school.

As soon as we returned to the Cape from Florida in early 1969, our lives began a downward spiral into chaos. The fact that my father did not love Dora anymore was an extremely bitter pill for her to swallow and she fought it desperately. Our mother wheedled, attacked, begged, and turned to alcohol as her ultimate weapon. Her dependence on Al was absolute and his rejection utterly devastated her.

The interception of a love letter—addressed to our father from a woman from Delaware—was an excellent reason to flip out. Al was out of town delivering artwork to galleries when Dora opened an envelope sent to the wrong house in error (upon our return to the Cape, Al moved to Truro, while Dora and Irene and I stayed in Wellfleet). As she read the letter through a veil of tears, our mother decided to act. Late that night, reeking of alcohol and weeping hysterically, she bundled Irene and me into the car (no seatbelts in those days) to drive the several miles to Truro. She was sobbing the whole way and drove like a demon. I had an acute fear that she might crash the car, but fortunately we got to Truro in one piece. As Irene and I stood uncomfortably by, our muttering and deranged mother rummaged through drawers, filling a bag with her family silver before drunkenly driving us back home. Later Al was incensed that she had violated his privacy. He angrily told Irene and me that the letter was addressed to *him*, not Dora, and that she should be prosecuted for opening his mail. It was just one more frightening thing for us to contemplate.

The most terrifying night of my childhood was on or around the day the divorce went through and Daddy came over to our house for dinner. I think this was an attempt to reassure us kids that, despite all the recriminations that were a daily part of the dialogue in our home, our parents could still be friends.

Me, under a tree somewhere

My mother bustled over a wonderful meal of duck, which was an exciting dish we had never had before. The table was lit with a romantic and seductive glow of candles, and our best plates from the gallery adorned each place setting. Thrilled that our parents were together again, Irene and I were on our best behavior. Every time our father laughed at our jokes and we caught our parents smiling at each other, I became more confident—everything would be normal again! My sister and I went to bed that night to the comfortable, familiar sounds of our parents chatting amidst the clinking of wineglasses.

Late that night, a terrible scream ripped through our darkened bedroom. We started up in our bed as another shriek rang through the house. It was horrible. We scrambled out of bed and ran downstairs.

Dora was pacing in the living room; she had her arms crossed across her chest and she was completely naked from the waist down. Her long hair, normally tied back in a prim ponytail, was loose and crazy; her eyes were wild with a look I did not recognize. Al was sitting on the couch with his head in his hands.

Dora looked at us and smiled, "Do you know what your father tried to do?" she hissed at us, "He tried to fuck me!"

Irene and I began to whimper.

Al started to say, "For God's sake, Dora..." but she whirled and screamed at him, "Shut up!"

Irene and I started to cry in earnest now. Dora looked at us with disdain and continued to pace the living room, all the while muttering about how our father had tried to seduce her. Al made a move toward her but, screaming at the top of her lungs, she lashed out at him, so he backed off. Irene and I begged her to go to bed and stop this, but we might as well have been playing hopscotch for all she cared. Al finally grabbed at her again, but with another shriek Dora broke away, yanked open the front door, and darted out into the night.

So, with our bottomless mother out roaming the neighborhood, Irene and I stood on the doorstep calling her name between hiccupping sobs, while Al went off in search for her. I can't remember which terrified me more: that someone would see her, or that she would leap out in front of a car and get hit... the end result being that someone would see her. The very thought of word getting out around town that our mother was wandering the streets half naked was simply more than I could bear.

Soon our father came back and ordered us to bed. He would find her, and everything was going to be fine. She'd just had too much to drink.

Irene and I crawled back into our beds, cried-out and exhausted. We managed to fall asleep, only to wake sometime later that night to another scream. I started crying again but Irene bolted up in bed and hollered at the top of her lungs, "Mummy, STOP IT!" Our father yelled upstairs to us both to shut up and peace finally descended on our shattered household.

The next morning Irene and I came downstairs warily. Our mother was nowhere to be seen, but Al was still there, and he helped get us off to school. It was the last time he stayed in our house. Dora pretended nothing had happened and we never brought it up again.

This was to be how we would deal with all the crazy events from then on; it was the equivalent of us all ignoring a huge pile of dog shit on the living room carpet. I became pretty adept at stepping over the pile, where Irene would take aim and kick it around from time to time. But no matter what happened, I had an irrepressible need to believe that somehow everything would be okay again.

This episode of insanity was a line of delineation that was as dark and deep as my mother's depression. I wish I could say that this was the last horror show Dora put on, but it was not. I was never able to truly trust my mother throughout my childhood and early teens. Gone was the person who loved and took care of me, and in her place, was an unstable stranger full of unpleasant surprises.

To say that my parents' divorce was acrimonious would be an understatement. My mother gave most of their shared belongings to Al, did not demand that he pay child support or alimony, and then became bitterly angry that he refused to send money. She claimed he lied, cheated, and stole from her, and that for the rest of her life she would hate his guts (I can attest that, until the day that she died forty years later, this remained true). The inappropriateness of her spilling this endless stream of bile on her little girls obviously never registered with her.

In the divorce my mother got the gallery in Wellfleet and Al the house in Truro. The gallery was soon put on the market because Dora felt that the only way to maintain her sanity was to get as far away from my father as possible. She bided her time running the gallery while Irene and I divided our time between her and Al. It was at this time, when I was ten, that my oldest sister Ellen took me to Monhegan for a summer without Irene, who stayed home and got her first summer job. It was the happiest summer I could ever remember.

Our Wellfleet home and gallery

I was unwillingly dragged back to Wellfleet in August to await our uncertain future. But one thing had changed; on top of everything else, I was now plagued constantly by a recurring dream of a small island in Maine. I knew that I would never, ever be truly happy until I could go back to Monhegan. While this brought me no happiness, at least I had something to yearn for. Yearning and hope helped keep my lingering despair at bay.

CHAPTER SEVEN ~ WESTWARD BOUND

I was headed out down a long bone-white road, straight as a string
and smooth as glass and glittering and wavering in the heat and
humming under the tires like a plucked nerve.

—Robert Penn Warren

Dora saw a therapist for a short time during the divorce. This kind man told her to go out and treat herself to something nice once the divorce was over... no doubt thinking that a new hat or some other trifle would make her feel better. Instead Dora went out and bought a brand-new, fire-engine red, Pontiac LeMans convertible; it was to be our chariot across the great United States. Early in the summer of 1970 she bundled a protesting Irene, our yowling Siamese cat Plato, and me into the car—and off we roared into the sunset. Destination: California.

Earlier, once it became apparent that Al really wasn't coming back, Dora got in touch with Ed, a divorced old friend of the family. At the time, Ed was living in Oregon, but Dora announced that he was coming east to visit. I'd last seen Ed when I was one, so I had no memory of the man; therefore, I wasn't prepared for the strange man who came into our lives. He was tall, bald, gangly, and comical, with one hand that had been mangled in a threshing machine when he was young. His favorite joke was to poke his partial index finger into his ear, so it looked like the digit was sticking all the way into his brain.

I liked Ed because he was funny and kind to me, but Irene distrusted him. After that disastrous night of the divorce, Irene had decided to oppose everything our mother did. They were constantly at odds and Irene began spending a lot more time with Al in Truro around then. I always just went with the flow. It certainly was easier that way.

Ed was a heavy drinker, which suited Dora just fine. They stayed up late at night whooping it up and both looked pretty tired in the morning. Ed started telling Dora about California and soon that was all she could talk about. He was a traveling salesman for a seed company and his territory was the Northern Pacific coast, including Northern California, Oregon, and Washington. He mainly sold to large growers and he had a special fondness for the far northern coastal California area where Easter lilies were grown. It was also the home of the great redwood forests. I thought it sounded pretty neat.

Irene despised the idea of California and the West Coast. She didn't want to leave her friends, her school, and her father. I decided to take my mother's side in the argument and pretended I was excited about moving. Why I didn't go ballistic at the thought of once again changing schools is a mystery to me. Perhaps it was because I liked Ed, who had just bought me a pogo stick.

The trip across the country was definitely a trip. We met Ed in Buffalo and continued to Chicago, where we stayed with friends of his in the suburbs. There we lost our cat. Old Plato managed to squeeze out the back window of the car that night and, though we spent hours calling him around the neighborhood, he refused to show himself.

We hadn't had much luck with pets when I was small. We first acquired a Doberman who turned out to be growly and mean so my parents got rid of her and got two Siamese kittens my mother named Plato and Socrates. Socrates immediately started eating wool, which apparently Siamese do, so my father took Socrates out and shot him. Plato was never inclined to do anything that put his life in danger, so he was allowed to stay. Later my parents got a German Shepherd, named Baron Shadow von Warrior, a descendant of Rin Tin Tin (or so they were told) to guard our gallery after a few minor break-ins. But Shadow had terrible separation anxiety and would tear apart any room she was left in; she also had it in for poor Plato and tried to kill him every chance she got, so she lived out her life outdoors in a dog run and went to live with Al after the divorce.

We proceeded from Chicago at a slow pace through the endlessly flat Midwest, the scalding hot Dakotas, and into the Badlands. I remember peeking at Mount Rushmore and one memorable night camping at Glacier National Park, when a grizzly bear was trapped in a big cage right next to our campsite. While we were in Wyoming, we stopped at an old-time general store and I stuck my mother with a live cattle prod. Her violent reaction seemed (to me) to be way out of proportion to a harmless little joke.

I think my mother started to dislike Ed somewhere around Chicago, and her silences became increasingly chillier as we went west. While camping one night early on in our trip, Irene and I huddled together in our tent through a pouring rain, listening to our drunken mother ranting and raving, with Ed trying to calm her down inside their own soggy pup tent. Later we acquired a pop-up trailer that we towed behind the Pontiac and struggled to open at various campgrounds.

Ed was an amateur horticulturist. He was forever bringing the car to a screeching halt in the middle of nowhere, so he could point out various plants and babble long Latin names to us, which further got on Dora's last nerve.

Ed's daughter was working as a cook on a ranch in Montana, so we stopped there to visit. The sky really *was* endless, and we were invited to ride horses through those incredible hills. I tried to absorb as much as I could, knowing on some level that this trip was truly one of life's great experiences. We cut across Idaho and dropped into Walla Walla, Washington, where Ed bought a big bag of onions from one of his customers. Later he fried up a bunch of those Walla Walla onions in butter for us; they were delicious.

Ed lived in a trailer park near Portland and I thought his trailer was cool. I had never been in a mobile home before and the fact that it was so finished inside, with its neatly paneled walls, carpeted floor, and nice kitchen, made me yearn for a home of our own again. We had been on the road for weeks and were tired, dusty, and sick of each other. Dora soon informed me that the trailer was tacky, ugly and in very bad taste; the park also didn't allow kids, so we went in search of another temporary abode.

We ended in up an apartment complex, complete with a pool. Soon after we moved in, Ed's friends in Chicago found our cat. They air-shipped him to us. Plato arrived, yowling his head off in his crate. I loved our kitty. He was as old as I was, and I had missed him terribly. Soon after we got Plato back, I took him outside to a vacant lot across the street. He looked around a little and settled down in a crouch, looking like he was going to take a nap. Suddenly he darted forward and grabbed a mouse before I even knew what was happening. I let him eat it. I figured he deserved one little mouse after all he'd been through.

The pool at the apartment complex was a lot of fun. There were plenty of kids and school hadn't started yet, so it was a pretty busy scene; we thrashed and played with great abandon. Soon I met a little girl who lived on a farm across the street. She would come over to swim and one day she asked if I'd like to go to her house. I went for a visit and she showed me their cow and taught me how to milk her. I remember feeling awestruck as I grasped and squeezed the soft teats; I was in heaven.

Irene grew more and more homesick and finally my mother decided to send her back to our father. Around this time, we were getting ready to go to Smith River, California, where we would be looking for a place to settle down in the heart of redwood country. I don't remember if I was sad that Irene left or not; it was just another thing that happened in my life and I had to accept it. Her departure did catapult me suddenly into the status of only child. Irene became a stranger I would see only on infrequent occasions.

We arrived in the Northern California coastal town of Smith River (Pop. 500) and stayed in our pop-up trailer at a campground near the mouth of the river by the same name. The campground was called Ship Ashore, a tacky resort with a large beached boat that served as a gift shop. It had a campground, trailer park, and a motel with restaurant and bar. I remember it well because my mother and Ed spent quite a bit of time in that bar. Ed had a lot of friends in the area and everyone was a drinking buddy. Ship Ashore acquired some fame a few years later when a lone gunman climbed on the ship and started sniping at patrons and employees. He shot six and four died. I never learned why he did this, but we were living just a few miles away at the time, so my mother and I were terrified while he was still at large.

Me with my fishing gear and the Pontiac—Smith River

Dora found us an apartment owned by a crabby lady who looked *very* askance at our lifestyle. She demanded a large security deposit and specified NO PETS. We assumed she surely didn't mean Plato and shortly thereafter we sneaked in a couple of black kittens Ed had given us, as well as a Labrador retriever puppy. The animals kept us company as Ed's travel schedule meant he was never permanently in residence, but our landlady always peeked around her curtains whenever he showed up. The kittens were hellions, constantly clawing their way up and down the drapes. When it came time to leave, my mother was unable to get her security deposit back (no doubt due to the tattered drapes) so in a rage she told the old lady that the bed in the place was horrible. The landlady retorted that maybe that was because there were *too many people* sleeping in it.

Soon it was time for me to present myself at yet another new educational institution. I went to enroll in the fifth grade at Smith River Elementary School wearing my usual attire of jeans and flannel shirt, with my hair cropped short in my customary tomboy fashion. It didn't take long on the first day before I realized that I was once again out of place. The girls all wore dresses and their favorite game was snapping each other's training bra straps. When one of them felt down my back to snap mine, her eyes widened with surprise, "You don't have one?" was the incredulous question. I shrugged.

I went out on the playground for recess and a boy came up and asked me if I wanted to play. Unfortunately, he thought I was another boy and was horribly embarrassed when he found out I was a girl. All in all, though, I managed to adjust fairly well. While the kids weren't especially friendly, they were not nearly as cruel as the Floridians had been. I didn't make any close friends that year, but our upcoming move to the farm gave me plenty to do. I soon found that the four-legged friends we acquired were enough to keep me happily occupied.

The farm was one hundred acres of second-growth redwoods, located on the north bank of the Smith River. Ed had made an offer on the property without involving my mother, though it was supposed to be a joint venture. It was a small single-story house with three tiny bedrooms and an attached carport. There was a large dilapidated barn and numerous outbuildings, including a fairly new chicken coop.

The current tenants raised coonhounds and when Dora and I arrived to take our first look at our new home, they were still in residence—dogs and dog shit everywhere. Numerous chickens wandered aimlessly about the yard and it appeared that there was a family of at least ten living in the house. None of the ten was a particularly good housekeeper. We picked our way through the god-awful mess: unmade beds with stained sheets in each room, old food strewn about the tiny, cluttered kitchen, and a toothless old lady who warned us that the well went dry every summer. As we stood on the front step after our tour, watching the huge logging trucks go roaring by at seventy miles per hour, just a few feet away, my mother sarcastically muttered "Great, I'll take it." … But it was too late to back out. Soon we'd moved in and had to spend many weeks sidestepping dog poop until it finally melted away in the incessant rains.

Dora remodeling the house in Smith River

Ed had forgotten to mention that the Northern California coastal redwoods resided in a rainforest; I guess the fact that the place received about one hundred and twenty inches of rain during the rainy season had just slipped his mind. I'm not saying that it rained all the time, just ninety-nine percent of it. The small Smith River grew into a wild, roaring yellow monster that tore up whole trees and threatened to overflow its banks. I developed an allergy to mold and went around with cotton stuffed in my ears, constantly dizzy from equilibrium imbalances. We spent a lot of time indoors, where I played with the cats and Dora tried to figure out how to make the shack habitable.

Ed's visits were fairly frequent, and it seemed that every time he came was an occasion for a party. The music would be blasting; we'd be dancing away to the sounds of the then-popular musical *Hair,* or Pete Fountain and Al Hurt doing Dixieland jazz. I would parrot the lyrics to a dirty song on the *Hair* album, hollering at the top of my lungs:

Sod-o-my... Fellatio,

Cunnilingus... Pederasty.

73

Father, why do these words sound so nasty?

Masturbation

Can be fun.

Join the holy orgy Kama Sutra...

Every-one.

I had no idea what the words meant, but everyone seemed to think it was hilariously funny.

Other music we played included Nina Simone, who taught me about civil rights through her *Pirate Jenny* and *Mississippi Goddam*. I'm also pretty certain that I was the only kid in my fifth-grade class with Carl Orff's *Carmina Burana* playing in her head, while having only blank looks for her peers who were gushing over David Cassidy. Ed's daughter was studying modern dance in college and she would perform for us during her visits. Dora fancied herself a modern dancer too, and, to my acute embarrassment, would drunkenly stagger around trying to show off her talent.

My mother always drank too much at any gathering and would get into stupid arguments with everyone. I came to dread the glazed face, mincing walk, and forced smile that gave away her level of inebriation. Despite the arguments, it was marginally better for her to have company when she was drunk; alone, she tended to the maudlin. When we were in the apartment in Smith River I came home from school once to find her well into her cups. By the end of the evening she was writhing on the floor, crying and moaning about how much she missed our father and how she wanted to die. I was horrified and helplessly begged her to stop. Finally, to my immense relief, she passed out.

The one thing that I learned from this insane behavior was that we must never discuss it. It was a secret that I had to keep, and somehow, I knew that if I just denied the existence of my mother's drinking problem long enough, and hard enough, it *might* go away. Up to the day she died, I was unable to tell my mother how her behavior affected me. This denial, this dishonesty was so deeply ingrained in me during those years that to say that it affected my entire life would be a gross understatement.

Whenever the rains paused for a moment, I was out the door in a flash to explore my amazing new world. The land contained a small stream, which swelled enormously during the rains and dried up completely during the summer. In the fall, I could spend hours watching the salmon in the pools fighting their way upstream toward their rendezvous with procreation and death. It was also a full-time job trying to keep the dogs from rolling in the rotten, indescribably malodorous salmon carcasses.

North Fork of the Smith River (P.G. Holbrook)

There was a ten-acre pasture and a small orchard full of apples. Back when the land contained old-growth trees, a fire had swept through, leaving several upright hollow trunks that were practically big enough to live in. Eight-inch long, bright yellow banana slugs oozed along the forest floor and my curious hands soon became covered in their slime. One day, I found a red chicken that had escaped her previous owners. I scooped her up, called her Henrietta, and carried her back to the coop. She immediately began laying eggs and became as tame as any pet.

Speaking of pets, I managed to collect quite a few. During the two years we were on the farm I acquired a couple of roosters, several more hens, a duck, a sheep, a mule, and a Great Dane. Ed's Labrador retriever visited off and on too, and both dogs would follow me wherever I went. Alas, I never could convince my mother to let me adopt a cute calf I saw during a visit to a dairy farm. Both of the kitties Ed gave us were killed on the road; old Plato finally crawled off to die, and I never saw him again.

Summer rolled around, and the Smith River beckoned. She had settled down and became the crystal-clear stream that flowed lazily in the pools and playfully over the rapids. She was my best friend that summer and my mother let me run free with her.

I had found an abandoned young sheep that spring down the road from the farm. He was a yearling castrated male, a wether who, I suspect, had dodged a date with the butcher. He became my constant companion. Shep was not the smartest friend I had but he was sweet and uncomplicated. Often, we would go to the river together and swim; Shep wasn't afraid of the water and would follow me everywhere, wet or dry. His only bad habit was that he would try to mount anyone who was foolish enough to bend over in front of him. Obviously, his little operation hadn't taken.

CHAPTER EIGHT ~ RACHAEL MY ASS

They took all the trees and
Put 'em in a tree museum
And they charged all the people
A dollar and a half to see 'em

—*Joni Mitchell*

Dora decided that since we had a farm, then I should have a horse. We had gotten to know a ranching family through Ed and we went over to their place to check out their horses. In the paddock, my eye was caught by a pretty young jenny mule named Rachael. She was brown with black feet, tail, and mane, and a creamy muzzle. She had the classic black stripe down the back with the mark of the cross over the shoulders; this was purported to originate from the humble ass's role in carrying Mary during her pregnancy (I've never been convinced), but this mule was certainly no angel.

Rachael's ears were huge and fuzzy, her eyes large and sad, and I had to have her. Her owner told us that she was green-broke, which meant nothing to us Yankees, but he demonstrated riding her and I thought I could do it too. He delivered her in a trailer along with another filly on loan for company. I learned how to saddle my new mule and soon was riding her pretty well… except that she had one bad habit. I could never canter that animal without her making a sudden feint to the side, effectively dumping me every time. As long as we went a trot or slower we were fine.

A girl and her mule

Mules are a thousand times more surefooted than horses, and that was a good thing because Rachael and I spent a lot of time exploring the cutover timberland surrounding our property. During the early seventies, logging of the old-growth forest was still in full swing in Northern California. Logging trucks roared by constantly, often with only one or two enormous tree trunks on the back. Sawmills hummed with activity, their smokestacks belching the smoke of burning waste. The erosion and flooding was horrendous, and the logging companies made no effort at all to clean up their clear-cuts.

My mule and I would enter a spooky realm of torn-up tree stumps the size of small houses with masses of slash woven into impenetrable thickets. The earth was a moonscape of ruts and cuts flowing muddily to the river during each rain. Often, for no reason I could discern, there were huge, fifteen-foot-diameter logs left behind to rot. The wisdom of that time was that the resource would last forever, but the waste and devastation was sad and depressing. Rachael would pick her way through the mess as neatly as a cat; we covered many miles this way.

Across the street from the farm was one remaining stand of old-growth redwoods. These ancient trees were indescribable in their beauty and enormity, exuding a certain dignity that I have never felt in any other place. The floor of the forest was covered in moss and ferns and here and there I would discover a tiny clear brook bubbling down the hill. The sun would barely filter down to my level, but I could see the slanting rays stabbing through the canopy. It was amazingly quiet—except for an occasional bird cry, there was absolute silence; the massive trunks with their strange fibrous bark seemed to absorb all sound. I would sit or play for hours, dreaming that I was an Indian, living hundreds of years before white people showed up and ruined everything, and all that surrounded me was endless miles of this amazing forest.

"Loggers and the giant Mark Twain redwood cut down in California"
(N.E. Beckwith)

Finally, I would climb up on Rachael's patient back and head back to the farm. Those trees are all gone now, along with thousands upon thousands of acres of old-growth redwoods. They are replaced by second- and third-growth trees, which will never see that stately maturity before they are once again cut for decks and siding. The only old growth left is in the protected parks.

Ed was a card-carrying member of the Sierra Club, which we joked was a punishable offence in that area by imprisonment... or at least a good beating. He did impart a love of the trees and nature to me and we agreed wholeheartedly that the ongoing destruction of that unique and beautiful land was a crime. He signed me up as a member of the club and I remember being very proud of my membership card when it arrived. He warned me not to tell my friends about this because they wouldn't understand. Thus, we became partners in a secret subversive society. Hell, what was just one more secret?

Redwood logging train near Eureka, California, ca. 1909

There was a small county park abutting the farm property, and Shep and I would wander over there from time to time to see who was camping. One day I met a young fellow who was living in his car. Jonathan was a bearded hippie with long dark hair and dreamy pale blue eyes. He was about twenty-seven years old, and for some reason he befriended this grubby twelve-year-old girl with her goofy sheep.

Jonathan reminded me of my oldest brother, Will. We'd had a lot of fun with Will when he visited us back on the Cape; he was bookish and very intelligent and did not think that any subject was too difficult to discuss with his two littlest sisters. Will had a black VW bug and we would pile in and go to the beach or ponds to swim. There he would tell us about thermonuclear warfare and other fascinating subjects. He was into inventions at that time, so he had us drawing up various diagrams of great inventions that were going to make us rich. The only one I remember coming up with was a pooper-scooper that had paddles that turned like a water wheel and would magically scoop up poop as you pushed it around the yard. I'm still shocked that we didn't get rich off that one.

So, I was very pleased when I met Jonathan in Ruby Van Deventer County Park. When I think back upon that relationship, I realize that his befriending this little girl who crept out of the woods smelling strongly of lanolin was an extremely kind act; he became a homeless big brother for me. We fished and swam in the river, built campfires, and while I watched him cook his beans, we would discuss the world, the Vietnam War, and he would tell me about his favorite movie, *Easy Rider*. Jonathan's obsession with that movie likely stemmed from his identification with, in his words, the brave bikers killed by rednecks for the simple crime of being born free. By his example I decided to be a vegetarian (except for eating the fish I caught) and I learned some very interesting theories about authority, pigs (the human kind), and the counterculture.

Once we were both lying on our stomachs on the river's beach, staring into other's eyes, and he told me wistfully that if I were only ten years older he would have liked to date me. I kind of squirmed at that one but he dropped the subject and we stayed friends. Of course, I'd told my mother all about Jonathan and she became faintly alarmed that I was fraternizing with an older man who was living in his car. She insisted that she meet him if she was going to sanction any further involvement on my part.

At that time, Ed had decided to buy a couple of beef steers from the Seventh Day Adventists who lived down the river. Now Seventh Day Adventists don't eat meat but for some reason it was okay for them to raise beef cattle... don't ask me why. The steers were rangy, half-wild things, with little in the brains department, but I was determined to tame them. After chasing them endlessly around the pasture one day I finally got them cornered, but instead of becoming my new friends, they both burst through the fence and ran off into the woods.

Now I was in big trouble, so I ran home to tell my mother that the cows had somehow mysteriously escaped. Dora and I went out looking for our steers, which had headed for the park. At some point we were chasing them down the road when Jonathan showed up. He joined in the chase, but the cows were faster and smarter—so we finally had to give up.

Jonathan turned to my mother, extended his hand and with a sweet smile said, "Holy cow, am I glad to meet you!" They were immediate friends from that point on and I was happy because I could bring him home to get into long philosophical arguments with Dora. He brought his *Easy Rider* album and we played *Born to be Wild* over and over again on our record player.

Ed's visits became less frequent. My mother had decided a while back (like about twenty minutes after we started the trip west) that she and Ed had very little in common. His friends were redneck farmers and salesmen, and she quickly came to despise all of them. He had absolutely no interest in her Edgar Cayce books, and they got into arguments about even the most trivial things.

My mother was engrossed in metaphysics at that time (a passion that I never shared). It was an interest that stayed with her for the rest of her life. She begged me to read Cayce's interpretation of the Dead Sea Scrolls and his theories about the lost city of Atlantis, but I could never get into it. I preferred to read about animals and I quickly devoured all of Gerald Durrell's books on Greece and zoo collecting trips around the world. His book *My Family and Other Animals* was my all-time favorite.

Jonathan, however, shared my mother's interests and would bring Dora books with strange titles like *Be Here Now* or *Autobiography of a Yogi*. They had long discussions about yogis, gurus, and Zen. Unfortunately, Ed didn't know Zen from zebras, so things continued to go downhill in that relationship.

At one point we became acquainted with a friend of a friend of Ken Kesey, the famous author of *One Flew Over the Cuckoo's Nest,* and we made a pilgrimage up to Kesey's property in Oregon. I had just read *The Electric Kool-Aid Acid Test* by Tom Wolfe (one of my mother's books that I half-understood at the time) and suddenly right there in front of me was Further, the famous psychedelic bus that Kesey and his Merry Band of Pranksters had driven across the country. Unfortunately, to our great disappointment, Kesey wasn't home that day but as usual, I was entranced by the farm animals they had running around the property.

Further (Joe Mabel)

Things finally took a turn because I wanted a big dog. I was studying dog breeds and decided that a Great Dane would be just the ticket, so we started looking around. Soon a woman brought a young bitch over for us to look at. This dog had a definite problem with her hind legs, which were badly malformed. Fortunately, my mother insisted we take the dog to the vet before purchasing her, where we found out that this poor animal had been grossly malnourished and was crippled for life. In an attempt to get us to buy the dog before we had her vetted, the seller put my mother in touch with the man who owned her dam. My mother called the fellow and as I listened, I noticed their conversation soon departed the topic of Great Danes and continued on in vastly different directions. My mother invited this stranger over for dinner and, as she hung up the phone, she sighed in a dreamy way, "What a fascinating man…"

The man who came to dinner on his motorcycle was a tall, handsome fellow in his fifties with a deep voice and captain's beard. He had a funny sense of humor and his name was Phil. Phil, like Ed before him, liked to drink… a lot. He was passionately into metaphysics and after a short stint with Scientology, he became a lifetime member of Eckankar (known as "Eck" to its followers). Now, don't ask me what Eckankar is because it's one of those strange quasi-religious-cult groups that I was never able to grasp; even Dora thought it was pretty bizarre.

My mother quickly fell for Phil like a ton of bricks and they embarked on a party that night that was still going strong when I went to bed.

I was very disconcerted to see that Phil was still there the next morning, sleeping in my mother's bed. After he roared away on his bike, I confronted Dora; I liked Ed and had come to think of him as my stepfather over the past year. My mother's two-timing was very confusing for me, but she airily waved me away, saying that Phil was just "too fascinating" and there was no question that they had a deep connection with one another. I asked her what about Ed, but she dismissed him with "Oh, I'm sure he's got another girlfriend in Portland." So, it was Phil when Ed was away and no Phil when Ed was around... yet another uncomfortable deception that my mother and I embarked on together.

Phil was divorced, and he had a little house perched on a hillside overlooking the ocean just a stone's throw from the Oregon state line. I have no idea how he made a living, since it seemed that he didn't work. He made no secret that he had another girlfriend down near Eureka, which antagonized my mother to no end. I thought this implied a bit of a double standard on her part, but kept my mouth shut.

The parties continued with Phil, Jonathan, and various other young friends of Jonathan's, or, alternately, Ed, Jonathan, and other friends of Ed's. I would slink into my bedroom early to avoid the sounds of merriment that rang through the house. It was a very lonely time for me. My mother was either in bed smoking and reading a book, or getting drunk with her cronies. They were all nice to me though and I learned to act very grown up, quickly donning the mantle of precociousness that many only children acquire.

We did eventually purchase a Great Dane, whom we named Bruno. He was a large gangly beast with very little brain. He grew distrustful of other kids for some reason and always rushed at them barking and snarling; this was pretty disconcerting to say the least. During my memorable twelfth birthday party, with about a dozen little girls in residence, Bruno got out of his pen. From all the screams that ensued I was sure we would have some pretty remarkable carnage. Fortunately, I was able to grab him before he devoured anyone.

My Great Dane, Bruno –Smith River

My mother was getting increasingly unhappy with life in the boondocks and was chafing for another geographical cure. She was on the outs with Ed and was frustrated that Phil was unwilling to make any sort of commitment. In addition, she began drinking earlier and more frequently throughout the day.

I was saddling up my mule Rachael to go for a ride when Dora came weaving down to the pasture, obviously intoxicated. She announced that she wanted to ride Rachael, so I obligingly handed the reins over to her. She swung up onto the saddle and immediately Rachael bolted. The damned mule went into a fast canter and then suddenly did her annoying sidestep—while Dora continued on straight-ahead and then plowed face-first into the ground.

A van was going by on the road and the driver saw the mishap and slowed down to see if everything was alright. I cheerfully waved to them as I walked back to where my mother was lying in the grass. When I got closer I saw that she was holding her wrist, which was grotesquely misshapen. I ran back to the stopped van waving my arms frantically and told them my mother was hurt. The man and wife got out, helped Dora into their vehicle, and drove away to the hospital, leaving me standing there frightened and bewildered. Dora yelled to me as they were driving away, "Call Phil!"

Dora and Rachael –Smith River

I ran home and picked up the phone only to find that our nosey, gossipy neighbor across the street was using the party line. I asked her in a quavering voice to please hang up because I had an emergency. She did, but I immediately heard her pick up the phone again as I dialed Phil's number. I told Phil that my mother had fallen off the mule and broken her wrist. He said he would be right over. Soon he appeared, putt-putting up on his motorcycle with a small bag of ice on board. I explained that Dora was at the hospital, so we drove over there in the Pontiac.

Dora had her wrist set and placed in a cast. She recounted her exciting ride to the hospital, saying that soon after the Good Samaritans had picked her up, they told her that they were Christian fundamentalists. They then proceeded to pray for her. Her predictable response was to faint dead away. When they arrived at the hospital, she was taken to the emergency room and the doctor asked her how she broke her wrist. In typical Dora fashion, she told him she fell off her daughter's ass.

There were a lot of Jesus freaks (as Jonathan instructed me to call them) in that area. The preponderance of the kids in my school belonged to some form of fundamentalist Christian church. Though it was the early1970s, Smith River was kind of stuck in the fifties. The ladies all wore polyester pantsuits and hairspray was a staple. The only social activities were the churches or the bars.

Once when I was playing down by the pasture on an Easter Sunday, a Volkswagen bus came barreling by at about eighty miles an hour, nearly knocking me off the road. I recognized a kid from school in the car and asked her the next school day why they were driving so fast. She sniffed that they were late for church. The irony of almost running me over while going to church never seemed to enter her mind.

FLAT ASS CALM

CHAPTER NINE ~ DIRTY OLD MEN

Sex at age ninety is like trying to shoot pool with a rope.

—*George Burns*

Irene arrived to spend the summer at the farm with a whole new body. She was now fourteen and had the curves to show it. Immediately she took charge of Dora and me, much to our annoyance. She bossed me around and argued with Dora and soon I was counting the days when she would go back east. Irene was attending a boarding school in Maine on scholarship, where my oldest sister's husband was teaching math, thus relieving both my parents of the responsibility of caring for her during the school year.

We had fun riding horses and my mule that summer too, but Irene's interests did not lie where mine did; she had no use for the woods and playing with dogs and sheep.

Irene was interested in boys.

Chris, a friend of Phil's kids, was very cute fifteen-year-old boy who came to visit us. My mother naively thought it would be nice for us to have a companion of Irene's age around. That night she gave us all permission to go camp down by the river.

Irene, Chris, and I brought our sleeping bags to the campsite and lit a nice fire. I crawled into my sleeping bag and Irene and Chris crawled into theirs. Only I noticed that for some reason they were both sharing one bag. Immediately they started making out... while I watched. I was repulsed, fascinated, and outraged that they were doing this right in front of me. I covertly observed them having sex (what little I could see of it with the sleeping bag in the way) until I fell asleep.

The next morning, I got up early and ran home. I wanted to tell my mother, but didn't know how. She could sense something was up though, and after very little prodding, I finally blurted out what I had seen. She listened with dismay to my sordid tale. I begged her not to tell Irene that I'd tattled, because I *knew* that Irene would kill me. Evidently Dora agreed that my life was in danger because instead she told Irene that she had just happened to wander down to our campsite that night and was not happy with what she saw. Chris went away, never to be seen again and Irene fumed. Irene confided in me that Chris thought I had told on them, but that she had assured him that Amy would *never* do such a thing. The illogicality of my mother visiting the campsite and then simply walking away while they were humping like bunnies seemed to escape her. I kept my fingers crossed, praying she would never find out.

When I was in the fifth grade I wrote the following essay on love:

Tuesday, March 30, 1971
LOVE
By Amy M.

Love is a thing that swells up inside a animal when he has met another animal of another sex that he especially likes. In man, love usally comes and goes as he is young. Then he will find a woman whom he loves more then all of the others. This one, in most cases, he marries and they may eather have children or be divorsed (or both). Seven out of ten familys these years are being divorsed because of family quarrels.

In animals (mammles) they will usally have separate mates each year or they will have the same one each year. In some cases two males will fight over a female. They will reproduce rapidly each year and eventually will die or be killed by hunters.

I was already having problems with intimacy due to my crazed family life and I wanted nothing more than to put sex away for about fifteen or twenty years... maybe until I was about thirty or so. But it did rear its ugly head several times during my childhood and it seemed like Irene was usually involved somehow.

Me in Smith River

Back during the idyllic Cape Cod days, when I was about nine years old and we were still a happy family, an elderly gentleman by the name of "Pop" lived nearby us in Truro. Pop, an old man in his eighties, was very kind to little girls. He had a garden and he would give us vegetables to take home to our parents. He also had a sign in his garden next to the melon patch that said; "One of these melons is poisoned. I know which one. Do you?" He assured us that he didn't *really* poison the melons but just wanted to stop the local kids from stealing them. Exactly why he was telling us local kids this was unclear.

One day my friend Cathy and I found Irene and Cathy's sister in a great state of excitement.

"You guys have *got* to go to Pop's house and ask to play his piano," they told us.

"Why?" I asked.

"Just do it and you'll find out," was the cryptic answer. Then they exploded into giggles and ran off.

It seemed like no big deal; some of the neighbors gave us cookies and candy when we visited, and I figured Pop was likely no exception, so we dutifully went up to his door and knocked. He invited us in and showed us into the piano room. His house was small with lots of knick-knacks and a strong smell of old man.

The piano faced a wall across from the door and we sat down on the bench, wondering when the treats would make their appearance. Banging away at the keys was quickly becoming pretty boring and I was starting to wonder why we were there, when Cathy glanced over her shoulder and quickly hissed at me, "What's he *doing*?"

I glanced over my shoulder and saw that Pop was playing with some sort of soft pinkish thing that was sticking out of his open pants fly. Now the only penises I had actually ever seen up to that day would have been attached to a very small boy, such as Cathy's younger brother, so I was unable at first to associate this large flaccid item with *that* portion of the human anatomy. However, it finally dawned on us what was going on and, being typical nine-year-olds, we giggled.

This soon became a very daring and risqué adventure for us. It also involved an element of danger, I mean, who knows what that dirty old man would *do* to us if given a chance? Judging from the permanent limpness of his Mighty Johnson, I now think that the danger was probably pretty minimal. After all, this was thirty years before Viagra. However, the corruption of our young minds was certainly an issue here, so we eagerly jumped in with both feet.

It sure beat looking for box turtles.

We continued to go have piano lessons, sometimes Cathy and me, sometimes Irene and Cathy's sister, and sometimes all four of us. These "lessons" invariably consisted of us sitting and giggling at the piano while old Pop diddled himself.

Irene had the nerve to ask questions of this creepy old fart and he told her that the man's penis was somehow inserted into the woman and that both parties actually liked it. She importantly relayed all this information to us to digest. It sounded really disgusting to me.

Finally, Irene decided to escalate the whole thing by writing a note one day that said, "We want to see you naked", which she crumpled up and threw in the wastebasket in the piano room. Of course, Pop immediately found the note and told us come over that evening after dark for a real show. Now this was seriously scary stuff and I begged Irene not to go, but she not only insisted on going, but also made it mandatory that we *all* go. I didn't want to be a scaredy-cat, so that night we all trooped over to Pop's house.

We had agreed beforehand not to go inside. Instead we planned to only taunt him from out by the road. He asked us to come in and we said no. To my horror, Irene then shouted for him to take his clothes off. The next thing we knew the front door opened and there, framed in the doorway, was the elder Mr. Pop in all his naked, wrinkled glory.

Unfortunately for Pop, his grand appearance at the door coincided with a car emerging from a driveway opposite his house. We watched with stupefied amazement as bright headlights splendidly illuminated the old man for several seconds before he could get his wits together enough to duck out of the way. We ran home laughing our heads off.

That was our last encounter because Cathy finally broke down and confessed to her mother, who then told our parents. I was actually pretty relieved that we all were forbidden to ever see him again. Not surprisingly, it was at this time that the detestable "no playing on Sunday" rule came about.

Strangely enough, a year or so later when we were in Florida, Irene and I were playing at the beach and, to our astonishment and disgust, there in front of us was *another* old man playing with his limp penis for us to see. Understandably, I was beginning to wonder if all old men did this.

So that was my stunning introduction to sex. I did figure out a lot more about it later. When I was about fourteen I would baby-sit for a young couple in Mendocino and they had in their bedroom a copy of *The Joy of Sex*. This I devoured while my little charges were sound asleep (actually I only looked at the pictures). I found all that pubic hair to be pretty off-putting. I couldn't even *remotely* picture myself doing that stuff and wondered why Irene liked it so much. Dora also had a book called *An ABZ of Love,* kind of a Kama Sutra in dictionary form. Other than learning the real meaning of Latin words like cunnilingus and fellatio (acts which were, by the way, *totally* gross), the book didn't make a huge impression on me.

Dora had a prudish approach to the subject of sex, which was the one taboo that, as a recovering Catholic, she was never able to shake. I never remember her discussing it with me at all. I do remember her telling me once that she didn't care for sex and she obliquely blamed her divorce on this. I learned about menstruation from a film at school and was very embarrassed when I had to ask my mother to buy me sanitary napkins. She acknowledged the request with an offhand, "Oh, so you've started," and that was that.

When we first moved to Smith River, I did manage to get together the courage to ask my mother for a beginner's bra, which all the girls were wearing, but by the time she finally got around to buying me one, a whole year later, I had already made up my mind that I would go braless.

I had entered the counterculture.

CHAPTER TEN ~ REBEL WITHOUT A CLUE

*The only people who ever called me a rebel were
people who wanted me to do what they wanted.*

—*Nick Nolte*

I climbed onto the school bus the first day of sixth grade in Smith River and immediately noticed a new girl. She was plump and plain, with short brown hair, a pug nose, freckles, and, most importantly, she was wearing work boots. Up to this point, I was the only girl in Smith River Elementary School who wore non-girlish footwear, so I was instantly interested. I sat down beside her and found out her name was Janet. She lived on High Divide, and she loved lizards. Well, that clinched it. Janet and I became buddies.

Janet's family was the first to move to the High Divide, a stretch of ridge running along the top of the coastal range that formed the backdrop of the Smith River coastal plain. When you drove up the long winding dirt road to reach High Divide, you found yourself quickly departing the lush, green, redwood rainforest; as you gained altitude, the scenery changed to Ponderosa pines, manzanita brush, and dry rocky soil. Lizards darted under rocks, vultures floated way up high, and you were in a whole different world.

Ed would often bring us up there to show us the beauty of the place. He bitterly complained and made ghastly anti-Semitic remarks about a Jewish land developer who had subdivided the land into lots and was trying to sell them off. It seemed unlikely to us at the time that anyone would ever live there, where no utilities were available, and it was a long, difficult drive up to the top. The logging trucks used the single-lane dirt road too, often barreling down the mountain at breakneck speed; God help you if you were in the way. But we were in the thick of the back-to-the-land movement in those days, and though it took longer for it to trickle into far Northern California than other parts of the state, trickle it did. Janet's family was at its head.

Redwood Logging Truck (Thomas Sennett)

Janet's family consisted of her mother, father, two uncles, her two younger brothers, and two German Shepherd dogs. They lived in army surplus tents erected on platforms. It gets cold in the winters on the High Divide—unlike in the river valley where I lived. While it was arid and got little snow, the temperature did go below freezing at night. The idea of living in a tent was pretty daring and I couldn't wait to visit them.

Janet's mother was a lady named Myrna. She was tall, lean, and dark haired, with thunderous eyebrows and a definite no-nonsense attitude. Myrna's husband, Doug, (a "longhair", as Jonathan had instructed me to call the hippies) was a handsome, sweet-natured guy. They were getting ready to build a log cabin on their land and drove old beat-up trucks. I have no idea how they made a living. I seem to recall that Myrna had some sort of trust fund that kept them going. Soon their whole family became acquainted with my mother and our friend Jonathan (who had moved out of his car into an apartment and was working in a sawmill) and we all became friends.

Myrna was not afraid of anything. After the third time she was run off the road by logging trucks (with her two-year-old son in the truck with her) she decided to take action. She calmly parked her truck in the middle of the road, pulled her shotgun out of the cab, and waited for the next truck to come down the hill. She pointed the gun squarely at the startled trucker's face and told him to tell his buddies that the next time she was run off the road, she was going to take a logging truck with her. They left her alone after that. My mother said that Myrna had the biggest balls she'd ever seen on anyone, man or woman.

Janet didn't inherit any of Myrna's spunk; she basically just followed me around and did what I did. She wasn't the brightest bulb in the chandelier, but we had fun hunting lizards and playing with the dogs and horses. She even backed me up when I made an ill-advised decision to dress up as a tree for Halloween, but she simply wasn't able to understand my first foray into anti-authoritarianism.

To place this in context, remember that this was 1972, still the height of the Vietnam War. My entire childhood had been marked with watching the body counts each night on the CBS Evening News with Walter Cronkite. My new, older hippie friends were all rabidly anti-war and their views became my views. However, in Smith River, California—a place where women still wore beehive hairdos—it could be very difficult to adequately express one's outrage over the current state of affairs. After thinking about it long and hard, I hit upon a way to make my mark: I would refuse to salute the flag at school.

I walked into my classroom one day and when everyone rose to salute, I stayed in my seat. Janet also stayed in her seat, not because she knew what this was all about, but because I told her to. Of course, the teacher challenged us, so I told him that I did not feel it was appropriate to salute the flag of a country that was sending thousands of its young men to be slaughtered in a senseless war. I knew I had impressed him because he immediately sent us to the principal's office.

At the principal's office Janet quailed and told the principal that she really didn't know why she wasn't saluting the flag and she promised not to do it again. They sent her back to class. I held firm however and my mother was sent for to bring me home. She seemed pissed about the whole thing, but all of my hippie friends said, "Right on!"

Halloween Costume – Smith River

We reached a compromise with the school. I would wait out in the hall while the pledge was recited. I think that they felt it would be a poor example for the rest of the students if I were allowed to merely sit in my seat, so they had to make a big production out of making me leave the room each time. The kids in school called me a filthy communist. This is what their parents instructed them to say because none of us kids knew just exactly what a communist was.

I realized that those of us who were willing to stand at the vanguard for a just cause would be persecuted, so I was able to walk with my head high and ignore them. This heroic stance was somewhat offset by the fact that I was mortified that nobody liked me anymore.

FLAT ASS CALM

CHAPTER ELEVEN ~ MENDOCINO

Hippies are so phony and fake.

—George Harrison

Toward the end of my sixth-grade year, my mother started looking around for other places to go. She told me that we had to leave because she was bored to tears with Smith River and the narrow-minded people living there. It was time for a change.

We started to make forays down the coast, stopping in Eureka, Ferndale, and finally climbing over the mountains into coastal Mendocino County. Once we left the coastal mountains, I had the feeling we were emerging, yet again, into another world. The Mendocino coast was barren grassland ending at steep bluffs, which dropped into the Pacific. The houses were New England in style, often with unpainted clapboards weathered a seal gray; the villages had white steeple churches; funny unpainted, vertical-slatted fences defined each yard. The trees were tortured by the wind into unnatural, surreal shapes, and nasturtiums tumbled over the cliff edges. It looked both bleak and compelling.

We stopped in the town of Mendocino, with its western-style wooden sidewalk running along Main Street facing the ocean. There was an eclectic mix of Victorian, New England, and Wild West architecture, dotted with wooden water towers. It was a funky little town back then, complete with head shops, craft stores, and longhairs everywhere; Dora immediately fell in love with it.

Mendocino Cliffs Late Sunset (Nelson Minar)

We drove around the area and my mother spotted a for sale sign on a house on a little street just east of town. We went in to investigate; it was a single-story ranch with four bedrooms, gardens, and a couple of small fenced pastures out back. We looked around and then went back to Smith River, where my mother wrote to the elderly couple who owned the house and made them an offer. It was accepted, so that fall we packed all our belongings, hitched a rented horse trailer to Phil's pickup truck, bundled in the sheep and mule, and started down the coast. I rode with Phil, who was driving the truck. My mother followed in the Pontiac with Bruno the Great Dane. The ride to Mendocino was uneventful, except that Rachael kept sticking her head out the trailer window and braying at oncoming traffic. We unloaded our stuff at our new home and Phil drove off. Bye-bye Phil.

School was underway, so I was dragged off to enroll in the seventh grade. Mendocino had a combination junior high and high school and I found myself in a very different setting from the elementary school I had just left. In fact, Mendocino resembled Smith River about as much as Great Danes resemble Chihuahuas.

At recess I was standing awkwardly alone, as I was wont to do, when a little kid of indeterminate gender, with longish blond hair and granny glasses approached me. I braced myself to be asked about my nonexistent religion when he said, "Hey, a bunch of us are going down to the field to smoke a joint behind the bleachers. Wanna come?"

I was so surprised that I blurted out, "Sure!"

He led me down to the football field where a small group of kids my age huddled together behind the bleachers passing a joint around. I took it when offered, inhaling a choking mouthful of smoke. I told myself that this was what really cool kids did, but actually I was pretty desperate to fit in at this new school… if smoking dope was how it was done, so be it. When the joint was finished, we all trooped back to class like nothing had happened. I did not get high the first time I smoked grass; it took several tries before I got a buzz on. I had many opportunities to assess my ability to feel the effects of THC because these kids all had a steady supply that they were taking from their parents and bringing to school.

Welcome to the Mendocino of the early seventies. My theory is that someone must have done a sweep of Haight-Ashbury in the late sixties and shipped a busload of what they dragged off the streets up to Mendocino. Or maybe some psychedelic school buses took a wrong turn on their way home from Woodstock. The hills were full of communes, ex-communes, and back-to-the-land attempts; there were free spirits galore.

The kids I went to school with were the offshoots of this great experiment in social revolution. They thought nothing of living in a home where nudity was the norm, everyone was high, and Mom shared her bed with different Dads. The town smelled of incense and hashish and, often as not, the waitress at the local café would be wearing a see-through blouse with nothing on underneath. I soon fit right in with the deftness of a chameleon, becoming one of the ragtag waifs who roamed that town alone or in little packs.

At age thirteen my body was making some amazing changes and I was very diligent about covering my protrusions with baggy clothes. Although some of my peers were already sexually active, I couldn't even conceive of participating in sex at that point. I did let my hair grow and got my ears pierced as a concession to girlhood, but also always wore an army jacket and black beret. This, I thought, made me look very bohemian and intellectual. Despite my attempts at camouflage, I was still the target of unwelcome approaches from older men. They would try to befriend me on the street, slow down their cars to catcall at me, and generally make me miserable because I didn't know how to deal with their harassment.

My mother and I liked to sunbathe on the back porch and we both wore bikini bathing suits when we did. Once I hosed myself off then lay face down. When I got up I left behind a wet imprint of my bikini and developing figure on the deck. My mother pointed to it and said, "That's the only part of you that men will see. Remember that." That was the only discussion we had on the matter (if you can call that a discussion).

Dora spent her time casting about for ways to bring in some more income. We subsisted solely on the proceeds of the mortgage she carried from the sale of the gallery on Cape Cod and I think this came out to about two hundred and fifty dollars a month. She must have had some cash too, because she always bought the houses we owned outright with no mortgage. Granted, they were cheap homes—I think the one in Mendocino cost all of twenty-five grand—but she had to wait quite a while before Ed bought out her half of the Smith River property and, with no child support from my father, we were strapped.

At some point Dora decided that she would become an interior decorator. She would be the first to tell you that she had excellent taste; she really did have a talent for converting very ugly houses into pleasant, interesting, and comfortable homes. In Smith River she spent a lot of time renovating that old shack we were stuck with and when we left, it was quite charming. In Mendocino she set about re-doing our house as soon as we moved in. She split her time between painting walls, installing bookshelves, studying her correspondence course on interior decorating (we called it "inferior desecrating"), and being hideously depressed. I could handle the first three but the fourth was really dragging me down.

Whenever I got home and found Dora sitting on the couch, her head in her hands and a decanter of wine in front of her, I knew we were in for a rough evening. As the wine level fell, she would invariably progress into weeping, crying, shouting, and making my life pure hell. It was an existence completely out of control and I was powerless to stop it. I finally got to the point where I just didn't give a shit. I became cynical and critical of most things. Gone was my usual boundless optimism and desire to see the bright side. Why bother when life was so fucked up? Besides, I had cool friends whom I could get high with now. This crazy home life coupled with my own maelstrom of hormones made Mendocino a dark and bleak time for me. For some reason I was simply unable to walk away and leave my mother when she was in this state. I guess I had an innate sense of responsibility toward her. Every time she embarked on these drunken forays into insanity, I stayed, almost as if I was chained there.

North Coast, Mendocino (Alan Schmierer)

Dora's next income-generating scheme was taking in boarders. A rag-tag stream of young men took up residence in our spare bedroom. A couple of them were memorable.

One, a shy fellow named John, was pretty insightful. After watching our mother-daughter interplay, he once gently asked us to try to "be nice." We looked at him like he was crazy. Our relationship at that point consisted of criticizing, judging, and putting down almost everything the other did. But for a short time, we took him up on his suggestion. My attempt lasted longer than my mother's, but if I learned one thing from John, it was "who in the hell am I to judge others?"

The next memorable character was a young Vietnam vet straight out of the war. He'd had enough time to grow his hair and develop a pretty nasty attitude toward Uncle Sam, which he managed to temper with large infusions of marijuana. He was soon thrust back out on the street again when my mother found out he was sharing his stash with her thirteen-year-old daughter. He left behind a junk automobile of antique origin in our yard, which really pissed Dora off. I would spend many hours sitting in that musty old car and even found a really cool Tim Hardin album in the back, under a mound of debris. The lyrics of one song, *Reason to Believe*, still runs through my mind:

Someone like you makes it hard to live

without, somebody else.

Someone like you makes it easy to give,

never thinking of myself.

CHAPTER TWELVE ~ A TROUBLESOME TEEN

*Adolescence is like having only enough light
to see the step directly in front of you.*

—Sarah Addison Allen

To escape my oh-so-happy home life, I would put Shep the sheep and Bruno the Great Dane on leashes and wander through Mendocino's downtown. We would cruise the shops and say hello to the proprietors. They soon all got to know me and would hide their potted geraniums from Shep. I would steal change from Dora's wallet and go buy penny candy at the store (it was in Mendocino that I got my first cavities). I met some strange characters in that town, but the sight of Bruno usually kept them at a distance.

We also explored the cliffs and small rocky beaches at their bases. Mendocino has the most incredible tide pools, all teeming with marine life, and I would spend hours hunting for bat and sun starfish, abalone, gaily colored nudibranchs, and sea anemones. Once I spied a bright orange octopus creeping over the submerged rocks. It was truly amazing the places I got Bruno and Shep to go; I spent a lot of time hauling them up and down precipitous cliffs and over slippery rocks.

I lost interest in Rachael; her frequent escapes from our minimal-security pasture finally prompted us to sell her. I brought home a puppy of indeterminate terrier heritage (her mother bore a strong resemblance to a mole) and named her Alice. Alice soon superseded poor Bruno in my affections and I think he knew it. One morning I walked sleepily into the kitchen only to step bare-footed right into an enormous mushy pile of shit that he had thoughtfully left in the middle of the floor. Bruno soon followed Rachael to a new home, leaving just Alice and Shep.

Mendocino Water Towers (Tobycat)

Alice went into heat and subsequently bore a large litter of multicolored puppies, each bearing a strong resemblance to a different male dog in the neighborhood. She was a lousy mother and I had to sit with her while she nursed the pups, or they would likely have starved. Later I sat on Main Street with them and found homes for each one, while Alice paid a trip to the vet to be spayed.

After I enrolled in school, I decided to try a foreign language and signed up for Spanish. The teacher turned out to be my next-door-neighbor, Mr. K. In a very short time I came to despise Mr. K. He was German and spoke Spanish with a thick Deutsch accent. He was also pompous (insufferably so, I thought) and frequently drunk in class; we all knew that wasn't coffee in the thermos he was constantly drinking from. Not only that, but he also drove a really ugly pink Ford Pinto.

From time to time Mr. K. would wander over to our house, always three sheets to the wind, usually when we had company, and start lecturing all of us about his bizarre views. My mother soon joined me in disliking Mr. K. One day we were trying to figure out how to get rid of this odious man when we heard a squealing coming from the back yard. We rushed out to find that one of Alice's puppies had gotten his head stuck in the slats of the fence surrounding Shep the sheep's pasture. After much consulting we decided to pour vegetable oil over the unfortunate animal's head to slip him out. Mr. K. barged in, as he was wont to do, and immediately took over, kneeling over the puppy to assume control of the rescue. Shep came up behind our German neighbor and calmly mounted the tempting rear end that was so thoughtfully presented to him. Shep was a big sheep, weighing well over a hundred pounds, so it took a little while to extricate Shep from Mr. K. and the puppy from the fence. It took a bit longer to control our hysterics. We finally got it straightened out and fortunately were bothered no more by Mr. K. After I left Mendocino, I heard that Mr. K's employment at the school ended when he drunkenly drove his car into the bleachers during a football game.

Mendocino Junior High had a definite hierarchy of kids. The school supported a strange mix of hippies, squares, and Portuguese Americans, with a few oddballs like me thrown in for flavor. We were all very excited when a couple of black kids moved to town and spent hours scheming how to become friends with them, but they were never a part of our rag-tag stoner group. In my grade there were a few popular girls we plebeians vied to be friends with. I was generally at the bottom of any pecking order and could never discern that magic essence that made one popular. I really tried, though, and did manage to carve my own niche into the junior-high society.

My best friend was Alison, an extremely introverted girl with a high squeaky voice and frizzy hair she always tied back in a ponytail. She had a dry wit and was also a tomboy, so we had fun together. Once I convinced her to help me with my drama club monologue where I was to play Stella DuBois in *A Streetcar Named Desire*. Allison merely had to play the part of Blanche, while I railed against her. Before class, we were fooling around on the school bleachers and Allison fell and badly twisted her ankle. Ignoring her pain, I told her she would be fine, and noted that she now had a great limp for the part. Only afterward, when her mother took her for x-rays, did we find out it was badly fractured, and she had to wear a cast for months.

My other friend was Rivka. She had a thin aesthetic face, long flowing hair, and knew from age two that she was destined to be a ballet dancer. She played Bette Midler albums and called me Daahling.

There was one immensely popular girl named Kelly. She was a little blonde hippie chick with a perfect body, and she lived with her parents and two brothers in a defunct commune in the woods. I followed her around like a puppy and hoped that somehow, she would notice and maybe be nice to me; generally, she avoided me and mocked me with her friends. In the eighth grade she found a boyfriend and she made no secret about the fact that they were having sex, which was totally cool with her parents. We all looked up to her and thought she was the most grown-up of us all, and we vied constantly for her notice and approval. She was that quintessential mean popular girl that most of us have experienced in school, unless of course we happen to be the mean popular girls ourselves.

Not too long ago I re-established contact with my old friend Alison and learned that when Kelly was eighteen, she went to Mexico with some friends to run drugs. Things went bad and she was murdered there. As it turns out, not all the popular girls do well in life.

In Mendocino I found my first boyfriend. Seth was fifteen, a year older than I. He had brown curly hair, a slim body, and a soft gentle face. He was into filming and had his own 8mm camera he used to make short movies. I was featured in several of these films; their plots generally went along the lines of damsel in distress gets rescued by a sheep, or some other similar vignette.

Seth also played guitar and we spent many evenings singing *Leavin' on a Jet Plane, Blowin' in the Wind,* and other sixties folk tunes. We had fun, and somewhere along the line started holding hands and kissing. Seth liked to kiss and neck but never went beyond that stage. He was a perfect gentleman and that was good, because I still was not ready to go any further.

Me at age fourteen

For my part I felt a detachment from the whole courtship process. I liked Seth and was certainly comfortable with him, but I wasn't in love and I certainly didn't feel any need to carry things to another level. Up to this point, only older men had expressed an interest in me, and I wasn't really interested in boys my age. But it seemed the thing to do at the time and it was somehow very sweet to be able to hold hands in the hall at school like so many other kids did. It was one more step toward achieving that mysterious condition: fitting in.

My drama club was preparing to do a production of Bertolt Brecht's *The Caucasian Chalk Circle*. I was to play the part of the milkmaid who was ravished by a stable boy. All I had to do was explain in a seductive manner to the new revolutionary judge how I was raped. The judge would then throw my case out and lead me off, presumably to participate in further sexual exploits. I think I did a pretty good job with my role (at least Dora laughed her head off). In the final production, the man playing the judge took a very firm grip on my bottom as he escorted me off the stage, surprising the hell out of me. Seth was also in the play with various bit parts and after the final show, we all went to a cast party to celebrate.

Immediately upon arriving at the party, I found a glass of red wine in my hands. I drank it. Suddenly all my old lectures to myself vanished like a puff of smoke. I had promised myself over and over again that I was *never* going to drink. I would *not* be like my mother. I brushed it all aside in an instant and promptly embarked on my first drunk. The events of that night are pretty fuzzy. I remember the fellow who played the judge putting a passionate lip-lock on me, but I soon blacked out and only remember coming to in the car that was driving us home.

The next day I felt fine and we all had a good laugh about my exploits. I guess I'd done a lot of hugging and kissing that night and poor Seth had to extricate me from all of it. I thought it was the most fun I'd had in a long time. My mother was amused and not the least bit concerned about me getting shit-faced-blackout-drunk at the age of fourteen.

I've got to say that I believe to this day that the only thing that prevented me from completely following the ruinous footsteps of my mother and various other ancestors was the education I got at Mendocino Junior High School. Somebody in that school system had their head in the right place, because our entire eighth grade class was forced to sit through a segment devoted to alcoholism, spanning a whole school quarter. There I learned it was a disease (a pretty novel concept in those days) and that the only way to halt the progression was to stop drinking entirely. I found out alcoholics were not just skid row bums, but people from all walks of life.

For the first time, it dawned on me that my mother just might possibly fit the bill. Having only been drunk once myself, I certainly knew I wasn't a candidate, but the seeds were planted, especially the ones that informed me that this was a hereditary disease. It was years before I was able to figure out that I was carrying this gene, but without this foundation in place, I doubt it ever would have occurred to me to change.

After having my head filled with all this information, I came home from school one day, and point blank asked Dora if she thought she was an alcoholic. She was taken aback but considered for a moment and replied, no, she wasn't, but that she thought she might be a *potential alcoholic*. I let it go at that, but I'd helped plant the seeds; I think this helped bring about the change in her drinking that was to follow later.

Dora did not condone my marijuana use in any way. To her this was a dangerous and illegal drug and my argument that it was less dangerous than alcohol made no impression. Consequently, I hid my dope smoking from her as much as I could. I preferred getting high to getting drunk, and I used grass to release me from the stress and worries of that time. She could tell when I was stoned, though, and her deadly silences and cold condemnation unsettled me. Her disapproval had no effect on my behavior, however, except to make me somewhat paranoid. Toward the end of my eighth-grade year I started skipping class to go out and get high. Somehow, I managed to keep it all a secret with forged notes from "Mom," and my grades did not suffer. Besides, I didn't need drugs to get myself in trouble.

Soon after we moved to Mendocino we had some new neighbors in the rental home across the street, a woman and her young son. Judy was a handsome woman, a fine-arts weaver in her thirties with platinum blonde hair. Sam was a brash, smart little kid, maybe two years younger than I, with freckles, curly hair, big glasses, and a bigger mouth.

My mother became friends with Judy and I hung around with Sam when there wasn't anyone else to play with. Sam had a couple of BB guns and we spent a lot of time fooling around; shooting targets or anything we could aim it at, including Shep. Shep had a thick fleece so it didn't bother him too much.

Our house would have had a nice view of the Pacific Ocean out the back windows, but someone had built an ugly pink stucco box-like house right behind us, effectively blocking any view we might have had of the water. Dora was constantly complaining about this building, which she found ugly and offensive to her sense of taste and harmony in the world. Hardly a day went by that she didn't bemoan the lack of a water view and the beautiful sunsets we would have had, but for that hideous pile of stucco.

One day, bored and restless, Sam and I and Shep the sheep and Alice the dog wandered over with our BB guns to the irksome pink house to look around. The owners were away, and the ocean-facing side of their house was a large wall of glass windows enjoying a splendid view. Shelves had been built right up against the windows inside and sitting on each shelf were many decorative glass bottles. Each bottle contained a different colored liquid, and the result was a rainbow of different colors.

This was just too tempting a target for me and, without even thinking, I took my BB gun and aimed it at one of those silly pretty water bottles. Sam watched with his mouth hanging open as I pulled the trigger.

There was a little "plink" and a hole appeared in both the window and the bottle behind it, whence a little stream of colored water spurted forth. Soon Sam joined me and before I knew it, we had fired holes through every bottle. The house resembled a leaky boat just pulled out of a magical rainbow pond, with little multicolored jets squirting merrily away. It was really very festive looking.

We were so caught up in our fun that it was a huge shock to see a man suddenly appear around the corner of the house. He was running toward us, waving his arms and yelling, "Hey! What the HELL are you DOING?!"

I wasn't a complete idiot, so I screamed, "RUN!"

We must have presented quite a sight: two gun-toting kids, a small dog, and a fluffy sheep running down the hill into the woods as fast as we could go. I took care to lead us in the opposite direction from where we lived. This might have fooled the guy, except for the troublesome fact that I happened to be the only person in the neighborhood with a pet sheep.

As it turned out, the man didn't have to find us because Sam was so shook up that he blabbed to his mother and the police were notified. A cop came to our house and filled out a report, charging me with malicious mischief—a misdemeanor. He explained that this would be on my record until I was eighteen. My mother was not pleased; I suspect the whole episode cost her a lot of money, which we could ill afford at the time. Worst of all, the BB guns were taken away, never to be seen again. Thus, ended my life of crime (at least the ones I got caught at).

Sam had an uncle Larry who would occasionally visit his sister and nephew in Mendocino. He was a tall, gangly man in his late twenties, with a large Adam's apple and almost no chin. The first time we met, he became hugely and inappropriately infatuated with me, another of my much-older admirers. Larry was a very friendly, funny guy and my mother loved him, so she completely condoned his public displays of affection for her thirteen-year-old daughter. He would tell me, and everyone who would listen, that he was my boyfriend. This relationship involved a lot of hand-holding, hugging, and chaste kissing. I simply went along with it, because I had no idea that it was wrong. Fortunately, the touching never went beyond hugs and kisses, even when my mother allowed him to share my sleeping bag when I was camping out in our backyard one night. Larry flitted in and out of our lives for several years, and he even taught me to drive when I was fifteen. Weirdly enough, he never lost his infatuation with me for as long as I knew him, though he finally did find another, much younger, woman to marry.

By our second year in Mendocino my mother was feeling once again that it was time to move. Maybe she was worried about the bad influence the place was having on me, but I think that she was miserably depressed and felt that another geographical cure was in order. Later I would tell her that the real problem was that she still had to take herself wherever she went. Even after I imparted this great piece of wisdom, she ended up moving over a dozen more times during her lifetime.

I finished my first year of junior high and headed east to visit family for the summer. My itinerary included Monhegan—where I would have my fateful first meeting with Thomas—and a trip to Nantucket to see my father and Irene. I was to return to Nantucket the following summer as well, and that year, while I was away, Dora made plans to leave Mendocino forever.

FLAT ASS CALM

CHAPTER THIRTEEN ~ NANTUCKET

There once was a man from Nantucket
Who kept all his cash in a bucket.
But his daughter, named Nan,
Ran away with a man
And as for the bucket, Nantucket.

—Dayton Voorhees

In August of 1973, after my stay on Monhegan, I headed for Nantucket Island, where Al had opened a new art gallery and Irene worked at summer jobs. There, I finally met my father's girlfriend, the very one who had lured him away from our happy family several years before. She was a very nice lady and I bore her no ill will. Even Irene got along with her.

I had a good time on Nantucket, where I found that despite being only fourteen, I would be served in the bars without producing an ID. I also discovered that I liked sloe gin fizzes. I spent all my free time riding a bike around the island, hanging out at beaches, and partying with my sister. There was one unfortunate incident, involving us stumbling around drunk in bushes that turned out to be poison ivy, but I survived, and I would return the following summer as well.

As I was learning about finer ways of drinking on Nantucket, Irene was, as usual, majoring in boys. One day, during my second summer on the island, she came home from a mysterious appointment and pulled me aside.

"I'm pregnant," she hissed into my ear.

I blurted out the first thing that jumped into my mind, "Do you know who the father is?"

"Of course I do," was the angry retort. "And we need to go to the mainland, so I can get rid of it."

It never occurred to me not to go with her.

Me in my father's sculpture garden on Nantucket (1973)

We came up with some lame excuse for our father, who was more preoccupied with his work than with his teenage daughters, and prepared for our journey. We boarded the ferry to Woods Hole the next afternoon, allegedly to visit a friend in Falmouth. What we really did was stick out our thumbs and embark on a hitchhiker's trip to Springfield, Massachusetts, the only place in the state where abortions were legally performed at that time, right on the heels of *Roe v. Wade*.

It was late afternoon when we got off the ferry and we had a hundred and fifty miles to cover.

First, we were picked up by a creepy young man in a Porsche. He explained to us that girls who wore provocative clothes really deserved to be raped. I was immensely relieved when he dropped us off near the Mass Pike.

It was pitch dark by the time we walked onto the highway. All I could think was, here we are, two teenage girls, thumbing our way to hell. It seemed like we stood there forever as the cars and trucks roared by and I was petrified the whole time. Oh yes, this was big trouble with a capital T.

First a semi pulled over and when we ran up to the door the driver looked surprised. He'd only seen one of us in the dark and was not pleased that he had a second girl along for the ride, which I imagine spoiled his plans. He dropped us further up the highway at his exit and we once again stuck our thumbs out at the traffic hurling by.

Finally, a car pulled over. It was a Cadillac driven by a middle-aged black man.

"What in heaven's name are you girls doing out here at this time of night?" he exclaimed.

We told him we were headed to the clinic in Springfield. He mulled this over as he navigated the Caddy smoothly out into traffic.

"I know a nice little motel not far from that clinic, so I'll take you there," he said kindly. "And don't you *ever* go hitchhiking at night again now, you hear?"

I was happy to follow his advice, though Irene had other plans.

The following day I paced in the clinic waiting room while Irene had her procedure done. I was nervous and worried and at loose ends, so when I spied a coffee machine in the corner, I figured this was as good a time as any to try it. I've always thought it was a little weird that my first cup of coffee was at an abortion clinic.

After Irene emerged, with only minor cramping, she informed me that, since we were on the mainland, we might as well take a trip up to Maine to visit some of her school chums. Again, like a dolt, I followed her back onto the highways as we hitchhiked up to central Maine to hang out and get stoned with Irene's friends. We stayed a couple of days and I tried to arrange a visit to Monhegan, but we were too pressed for time. Finally, we made our way, via thumb, back to Woods Hole and took the ferry back to Nantucket, where our father basked in blessed ignorance.

Al on Nantucket

CHAPTER FOURTEEN ~ DANCES WITH EURAIL PASSES

To understand Europe, you have to be a genius—or French.

—Madeleine Albright

At the end of my second Nantucket summer, Dora flew to Boston to meet me at my brother Will's apartment. Will's girlfriend at the time was a nudist, and she surprised my mother on the first morning of her visit by appearing in the kitchen completely naked, blandly asking what everyone would like for breakfast. But Dora was from Mendocino, where this was pretty much the norm, so she regained her composure with her usual aplomb.

I walked into Will's apartment and met up with Dora for the first time in several months. She was thinner than I remembered, and she immediately announced to me that she had quit drinking, had a new boyfriend named Nels, and that she and I were both going on a trip to Europe.

I was surprised because I was supposed to be starting school in a few days, but she airily brushed that off, saying that a tour of Europe was far more important and educational than the first half of my freshman year of high school. That was fine with me, so soon Dora had booked us passage on the *France*, a ship that was going to make the very last transatlantic ocean liner crossing from New York to England.

We set off for Europe on the elegant France. I remember little about the trip except it was gray, rough, autumn weather and I was slightly nauseated much of the time. Dora made me march back and forth on the decks, which was her remedy for seasickness. Meals helped, and oh what meals they were… the French cuisine was extraordinary. I was plied with alcohol in the fine European tradition and there were disco parties late into the night.

Postcard from The France

At one late-night dance event, Dora grew tired and left me to my own devices to dance with the young men. One of the ship's hands approached me and offered to walk me back to my cabin. He even held my hand during the walk back, which I found to be very nice of him. When we got to our cabin, where I was about to wish him goodnight, he pushed me up against the cabin door and simultaneously kissed me, pushed his tongue in my mouth, thrust his knee between my legs, and put his hand on my breast. I turned the doorknob and fell into the tiny cabin onto an astonished Dora's lap, as my "escort" beat a hasty retreat.

We docked in Southampton and began a totally unplanned and self-guided whirlwind tour of the British Isles and Europe, armed with a couple of Eurail passes and whatever our whim told us to do.

I barely remember London but we soon tired of it and decided to go to Scotland, only the train was booked. We were told, however, that there was room in a baggage car, so we spent a very uncomfortable night trying to sleep on a freezing boxcar floor. The very loud and very drunk Irishman yelling obscenities all night long just added to the flavor of the adventure.

We arrived in Aberdeen, but decided it was boring, so we went to check out the Isle of Skye because it sounded romantic. We arrived at the ferry on a dark rainy night with no reservations or clue where we were going to stay. We crossed over and were directed to a little house where a sweet little lady took us in, fed us warm food and gave us lovely soft beds with hot water bottles.

The next day was Sunday and we had no car, so thinking to get a ride to the other ferry off the island, we went out walking on the roads through a stark landscape that reminded me of Manana. I put out my thumb to passing cars while Dora walked along pretending she didn't know me because she was mortified that we were reduced to the horrors of hitchhiking. I was surprised by the incredibly dirty looks we were getting from the motorists, who kept passing us by.

Finally, an Irish fellow stopped and gave us a lift to the other ferry. He chuckled and asked if we'd waited long for a ride. I told him yes and I had been worried we would never get picked up. He explained that NOBODY hitchhiked on a Sunday on Skye; they were all very religious, God-fearing folk there, and they considered hitchhiking blasphemous.

We soon tired of England, so crossed over to France and used our Eurail passes to bypass Paris and go straight to Germany.

We had very little money for this trip, so we stayed at inexpensive pensions or on the trains with our passes. Different countries had different styles of accommodating passengers on their trains, and some simply resorted to a compartment with six bunks that men and women occupied. On our first overnight train ride, we crawled into our beds fully clothed; Dora was horrified when a gentleman entered the room and calmly undressed down to his skivvies before crawling into his own bunk.

We rode down to Austria and northern Italy, where Dora had some acquaintances she had met during a previous visit to Europe. Our picture albums at home featured some photos of a young woman and her two little boys. They were dressed in Tyrolian outfits, complete with lederhosen and dirndl dress; the woman's beautiful long hair in braids around her head reminded me of the Heidi books I read as a child. My mother had met this woman during her European visit shortly after the war, and they had continued to correspond over the decades. One of the sons had been killed many years before in an accident, but the woman, her husband, and their remaining son still lived in the area of northern Italy that had been part of Austria before the war. I also learned from my mother just before we showed up that the husband was formerly a Nazi SS officer, which, since my knowledge of WWII at that point came directly from *Hogan's Heroes*, really didn't set me back too much.

They were very kind to us, except the husband, who had a big scar across his face and, when he could be bothered to talk, grunted monosyllabically; pretty much how you would expect a former Nazi to behave.

We stayed in the Dolomite Alps for a while and then ventured down to Rome. Here I became acutely aware of the Italian men and how insane they were about young blonde females. Walking along sidewalks produced a cacophony of honking horns, whistles, hooting, and hollering, the likes of which I'd never experienced in my short fifteen years of life. I was mortified and frightened by the attention, and as usual, unnerved by the harassment. We spent very little time in Rome and while at the train station on our way out, I wandered off looking for a bathroom. I went down some stairs and found myself in a long-abandoned tunnel with a young man following along behind me.

"This is it," I thought, "I'm going to get raped and killed RIGHT NOW."

The man suddenly, inexplicably turned on his heel and walked away; I escaped with a pounding heart, vowing to never let Dora out of my sight again.

In Italy I noticed our train rides seemed to invariably follow the same pattern. We'd sit in a compartment with several other people and then everyone would light up cigarettes. Then the "discussions" would start with the passengers, which turned into an increasingly heated exchange in Italian and soon devolved into shouting and wild gesturing. Each time Dora and I would watch this display wondering whether they were talking about local or world politics, or perhaps just the price of milk.

We ended up in Sicily, staying in a horridly dirty place that the cab driver recommended, then we bolted off to Spain. By now we were getting tired and thoroughly sick of trains; we were filthy and our clothes were equally rank, since we couldn't seem to figure out how to get them laundered. So, we stayed briefly in Barcelona and did a quick trip to Majorca, so we could visit another island, and decided to head to Holland to catch a flight back home.

We found a flight that stopped overnight at Reykjavik, Iceland, with a tour. We thoroughly enjoyed Iceland, with its geothermal outdoor pools and friendly people. It was late November, so all we saw of the sun while we were there was its all-too-brief reflection off some far-off mountains before it set again.

When our plane landed in New York, I was enormously relieved to be home. It was my first experience with an extended stay away from my country and I never knew how much I would miss the good old U.S.A.

FLAT ASS CALM

CHAPTER FIFTEEN ~ CRESCENT CITY HIGH

All you need is ignorance and confidence and the success is sure.

—Mark Twain

Dora's choice of place to relocate was, strangely enough, Smith River again. Her old boyfriend Phil had decided to sell his little house overlooking the ocean near the Oregon state line and offered it to Dora for a song. She took it without a second thought and soon I found myself back in the land of redwoods... and rednecks.

I think the reason Dora fled Mendocino was because she finally had a wake-up call about her drinking. At some point while I was back east, she woke up in a ravine full of blackberry brambles with no memory of how she got there. This experience scared her enough to push her to attend her first AA meeting. I learned about this because she wrote a short essay about it; sadly, I have since lost it.

Along with her talents for recognizing good taste and how to run an excellent art gallery, my mother was also a pretty damned good writer. When she got inspired, she would fire off on her manual typewriter a work of prose about some crazy thing that happened to her that was always a joy to read. This is an excerpt from a piece she wrote about the time she went to see the Yogi Bajhan, which for some reason involved camping. My mother hated camping.

Dear Phil,

I arrived here yesterday evening with an empty tank of gas, six cents in my purse, and a hideous hangover. We're about thirty miles inland in incredibly beautiful country—mountains covered with good-sized second-growth redwoods.

After parking my car at the end of a long, dusty road leading nowhere, a four-wheel drive shuttle took me and my gear three more miles over God-awful trails to the camp site, where everything was unceremoniously dumped. The men camp on the lower level; the "activities" area and "couple" campsites are up a long, 90-degree road, in a huge meadow; and the "shakties" (that's me) camp another mile up the mountain, up a trail even a mule would find frightening. Steps carved in the mountain for footholds.

Of course, I always have to travel in grand style (not really, but I'd been told that I could drive to the campsite) so I had a huge tent up to Ringling Brothers standards, a director's chair (in case I have to direct anything) a typing table, typewriter, two large suitcases so I won't have to wash clothes while I'm here, a chaise, sleeping bag, pillows, ten books, two flashlights, peanut butter, crackers and half a watermelon, for God's sake! Plus, all the other little non-essentials. (At least I don't have a framed picture of Yogi Bajhan in my tent, as my neighbor has.) I finally got to the top of the mountain carrying only my purse, but that little maneuver took me about an hour and left me prostrate for another hour.

I missed din-din as a result, so I had nothing to eat all day, except your hangover tea early that morning. Made another trip down the hill for my sleeping bag and by the time I got back up here, it was completely dark and I couldn't find my purse which, of course, contained my flashlight. I finally collapsed in my sleeping bag in what later proved to be a gully on the side of the mountain full of rocks and crawling things. And mosquitos! Dear God. Of course, I hadn't thought of mosquito repellent, but I did bring my bottle of Chanel #5.

I like to think that I got my ability to write from my mother. She never had anything published, though we nagged her endlessly to do so. I guess she wrote simply for the joy of it.

When she finally dragged herself to an AA meeting, my mother decided she hated it right off the bat, but she did meet a man there, so it wasn't a complete waste of time. Nels was a sometimes-recovering alcoholic who caught Dora's attention at her first meeting when he loudly declared to the room that he fucking hated AA. They found they had a lot in common from that moment on and Dora informed me that Nels was the first man she'd ever met who had such good taste that it rivaled her own.

A somewhat taciturn guy of Scandinavian descent, Nels claimed that he never had a problem with alcohol until he was hit over the head while being mugged. The mugging resulted in a long coma from which he launched himself on a binge-drinking career that lasted the rest of his life. I strongly suspected that the mugging, done by two black men, served more as an affirmation of his lifelong racism than anything else. He did manage to stay dry for long periods of time and I never saw him drunk while I lived with them.

The good result of this relationship was that Dora gave up drinking too, and that nightmare period of her existence seemed to be over at last. Not to say that she was happy or satisfied with her life—that would be expecting too much. She still carried all the baggage and unhappiness that had been part and parcel of her drinking life, but she did it sober instead of drunk.

She remained engrossed in her metaphysics books and had an especially keen fascination with the Indian philosopher Krishnamurti (she'd given up on yogis). Her depressions never went away, and many days were spent in bed, her books and cigarettes always within reach. But her drinking had stopped... just as mine was taking off.

I blundered into high school in Crescent City, a small backwater twenty-five miles from our home. Crescent City's main claim to fame is that it was wiped out by the tsunami following the 1964 Alaska earthquake. It also had the only high school in all of Del Norte County, where we lived. When I enrolled in what was now my seventh new school, they looked askance at the fact that I'd missed the first semester of my freshman year, but I soon caught up in every subject, except math; I'd missed the first semester of algebra and decided to make do with basic math instead.

Paul Bunyan and Babe the Blue Ox, Crescent City (Jana Taylor)

The kids from Smith River whom I had left two years before were now part of the large group of twelve hundred teenagers attending that school, most barely recognizable in their new grown-up bodies. Janet's family had moved off the High Divide when Myrna had left Doug after he took up with a younger, prettier woman. Without my influence, Janet's allegiance had shifted to a group of kids a bit dull for my taste. After talking to her a couple of times, I quickly realized that we no longer had anything in common, so we drifted apart.

By this time, I was a complete hippie misfit: still braless, and wearing not an ounce of makeup. I sneered at the other girls with their anachronistic hairdos, high heels, lipstick, and nylons, as I sat cross-legged on the school hallway floor eating organic oranges and wearing clothes from the Salvation Army thrift shop. They, in turn, avoided me like the plague. There weren't any boys who interested me there either. They were either too immature or into cars; I didn't have a clue how to relate to them—nor they to me. I was actually painfully shy around almost everyone my age. Underneath my hippie-dippy demeanor, I was still a frightened and introverted kid. I could more easily relate to older people than to young, due to my mother always treating me as an adult, and our friendships with mostly young men and women in their twenties or thirties who also treated me as a peer.

I can't say that I enjoyed my time at that high school, but I had one learning experience that did stand out. One of my teachers would constantly exhort us to question things, even the things we were told on no uncertain terms were true. "Think for yourself!" he would constantly tell us; that being one of the most valuable lessons any teenager could learn.

My old friend Jonathan was still living in Smith River and he resumed his visits. However, Jonathan's interest in me seemed somehow different, his gazes held some troubling indicators that I was someone who might be considered as more than just the friendly kid he met at a county park. I became increasingly uneasy in his presence.

The main torture for me while I was in Smith River was the endless bus ride to and from school each day. The ride was over an hour each way. I had no friends on the bus, and I couldn't even read during the ride because it made me queasy. It became an endless grind of staring out the window at the same monotonous scenery of barren lily fields and stupid cows grazing in pastures, punctuated by stops to let on or off passengers. I was the first on and last off the bus, as the route ended at the California-Oregon state line where I lived.

The bus driver, an overweight lady in her forties with a beehive hairdo and nasty attitude, played the same few 8-track tapes over and over again. The sound of John Denver singing *Sunshine on My Shoulders* still makes me ill, and after the hundredth time of listening to Jim Croce sing *Bad, Bad Leroy Brown*, I was fervently and uncharitably glad that ol' Jim had died in a plane crash. I came to dread the ride with a palpable intensity, feeling the days crawl by with agonizing slowness toward the only dim hope in my life; the day when I would finally have my driver's license and be able to drive myself to school.

My sister Irene came to stay with us when I was in my sophomore year. She had found that she could graduate high school a semester early if she finished out in California, so she reappeared in our lives once again. Irene had as great a love for alcohol and marijuana as I, but this was outweighed by the fact that she had a very much cherished driver's license. She had saved some money from her summer job and immediately went in search of a car. She quickly found an old Datsun sports car at the local used car dealership that was just affordable, and immediately bought it. The thing dropped its transmission on the first trip out of our driveway and it was a long time, and many threats later, before we finally got the dealer to take it back in exchange for a large ancient International Harvester panel van of a lovely turquoise color. The Beast became our chariot to school and the home of many parties that Irene managed to put together from the dregs of Crescent City society.

With her new wheels, Irene never hesitated to stop for hitchhikers, no matter how grungy they looked. She met many new friends this way. Once she hit the brakes for a down-and-out looking guy with his thumb out, who suddenly materialized out of the mist. The old van did a full three sixty on the slick pavement before finally coming to a shuddering halt, miraculously facing the right direction. The hitchhiker ran up to us after our display of vehicular acrobatics and exclaimed, "Wow, cool!" before climbing on board for a ride to Crescent City.

Boys gravitated to Irene like flies to jam, and we spent many an evening tooling around the area with several passengers of the male persuasion and a rapidly disappearing case or two of beer on the backseat. I went along on all these forays, though I'm not sure why Irene invited me, maybe she just wanted to bring her pet sister along. I did manage to chug down my share of beer, and one evening after an especially hardy night out, I decided it was time take up driving on my own.

We had been hanging out in Crescent City with some older guys that Irene had found, and we were both pretty blotto from all the Blue Nun wine we had been drinking. It was time to go home and Irene took the wheel. Irene always managed to drive somehow, no matter how plastered she was, and it was sheer luck that we were never stopped,

132

especially given the fact that our area was a training ground for the California Highway Patrol.

She carefully navigated our way back to Smith River and we slowly chugged the Beast up the steep driveway to the house. When we got to the top of the driveway, we found our mother's car blocking the way, so Irene carefully pulled the Beast's parking brake and got out to move the Pontiac, leaving the van running.

I figured, what the hell, I could move the Beast ahead once the car was out of the way, so I slid into the driver's seat as soon as Irene vacated it. I had never driven before, especially this double-clutch monster, but I knew it would be easy; I was on top of the world at that point and needed only the will to find the way. I pressed down on the clutch, ground the stick into what I figured was first gear, released the parking brake, hit the gas, and popped the clutch. The van lurched ahead in an alarming fashion only to come to a grinding, sickening, and sudden halt, with its nose firmly embedded in the side of the house… right under Dora's bedroom window.

The following day's inquisition led to our only grounding by our irate mother. Other than that, we were pretty much given free rein. Soon, however, Irene graduated, and she took off for Cape Cod, leaving me once again car-less and victim to the crushingly dull and endless bus rides to school.

I finally managed to find a couple of girlfriends in high school; outcasts like myself, to whom I introduced the joys of marijuana and alcohol. We took some comfort in being social pariahs together and I even convinced one of them to come with me to Maine for the summer of our sixteenth year. I'd fixed up jobs at the store for us both, and my oldest brother, Will, would be out there to chaperone us.

Sarah was a beautiful, tall young woman with golden-brown hair and a face sculpted by her Native American ancestry. We shared the same birthday and were inseparable. She lived with her family in a log cabin on the bank of the Smith River, near Jedediah Smith Redwood State Park. Her parents were both born-again Christian fundamentalists, an ethos that Sarah did not share; I suspect she was attracted to my rebelliousness more than anything else. I was surprised her parents let her go with me to Maine, and I can only surmise that they were so wound up in Jesus that they overlooked the fact that they were sending their nubile young daughter out into the devil's own backyard... with very little supervision.

Redwoods in Jedediah Smith Redwood State Park, Crescent City (Miguel Vieira)

Not long before we were to depart, Dora decided to take a trip to the desert in southern California. Nels was filling her head with how wonderful it was there, and I suspected yet another move was on the horizon. Since the school year was not over, this trip meant that she would have to leave me in Smith River for a couple of days. She asked our old friend Jonathan to come over and stay with me, so I wouldn't be alone.

For the most part Jonathan behaved himself, allowing me to drive his car to school with my learner's permit, and going dutifully to his room every night at bedtime. But the last night of Dora's absence proved too much for him; he knew that time was slipping away, along with his chances of seducing me. He spent our last evening together attempting in every way possible to convince me to allow him to relieve me of my virginity. After all, it was just a burden and he was more than happy to take it off my hands. I declined. By then, I'd adopted a lofty idea that sex would be only consummated with the person with whom I was truly in love, and Jonathan, the now-older hippie in his thirties with stringy hair, just didn't measure up. I also had a secret memory of some handholding I had engaged in on Monhegan Island two years before, so I was willing to wait just a little longer.

The day finally arrived when Sarah and I were to leave. That June 1975, my mother put us on a plane to head back east toward my recurring dream. She was letting her youngest and most damaged fledgling out of the nest, long before I was equipped to fly solo.

FLAT ASS CALM

PART III

FLAT ASS CALM

CHAPTER SIXTEEN ~ SEX AND DRUGS AND ROCK AND ROLL

*Please allow me to introduce myself
I'm a man of wealth and taste.
I've been around a long, long year
Stole many a man's soul and faith.*

—*Rolling Stones, "Sympathy for the Devil"*

Sarah and I arrived on Monhegan Island in a bank of fog. June on the coast of Maine can be unpredictable, and that year it was mostly rainy and foggy. Sarah hated it almost immediately, but I was too much in heaven to notice. Finally, I was back on the island of my endlessly repeating dream. It was all there: the reassuring wharf, the cries of seagulls, my siblings' house with the charming antique windows and kerosene lamps. The stinky creek was there too, trickling out of the meadow onto the little swimming beach with sea glass. I could hardly believe it was real and I thought my heart would burst with happiness.

My brother, Will, was spending his summer on Monhegan working on the dissertation for his PhD in animal behaviorism from Harvard. It should also be said that Will had about as much interest in us girls as he did in the current fashions in *Vogue* magazine, i.e. zero.

Monhegan Idyll

We were completely on our own and made haste to take advantage of the situation. I immediately noticed the golden boy, Thomas, working across the street from our house stacking his friend's lobster traps. I was too shy to approach him, but gazed out the window at his tanned, shirtless torso and flexing muscles as he heaved the wooden traps into towering piles to be stored for the summer.

The next morning Sarah and I went to see the daily mail boat arrival. There was Thomas, standing on the slip talking with some friends. Thinking that it was now or never, I jumped down onto the slip beside him. They call it a "slip" for a good reason, because my boots shot out from under me and I landed flat on my ass at his feet. Laughing, he gave me a hand up and we became reacquainted. It turned out he was also working at the Monhegan Store that summer as a grocery delivery boy. Things were looking promising indeed.

Two days after we arrived our toilet backed up, so Will, Sarah, and I were forced to uncover the cesspool in the yard, and bucket out pails of congealed shit, which we furtively deposited at the Swim Beach's low-tide mark in the middle of the night. This did not improve Sarah's perceptions of the island.

Sarah and I experimented with cooking. Neither of us was very good at it—I excelled at pies made with crusts laden with lard, Sarah only knew how to make tacos. Therefore, we decided to fast twice a week to lose weight and forgo the annoying cooking problem. Fasting was a fierce test of wills and competition for us. We were both annoyed by our puppy fat and seduced by the ideal of a perfect Twiggy-like physique. I already had a pretty good all-over tan from sunbathing in the nude all spring back home and I needed to complement this with what we had been indoctrinated to believe was the female ideal: a curveless stick figure.

We were invited to our first party soon after; it was the usual drunken island affair with tons of alcohol flowing with great abandon. Thomas and I talked all night and I found him to be absolutely fascinating. I got very drunk and watched with bleary astonishment as Sarah got herself spirited off by the party's host for a steamy one-night stand. Thomas helped me home and abruptly left me at my doorstep after one small, very chaste kiss. I stood there swaying under the stars before stumbling off to bed—with nary a peep out of Will.

A few nights later, I accompanied Thomas on a walk up to the lighthouse. I was stone cold sober, and we didn't even smoke a joint together. We lay under the moon talking for a while, then we got up and, holding hands, walked back down the hill to his parents' cottage, which he had to himself that summer. Thomas lit a fire in the fireplace, and before I could even think, "This is it!" he quickly proceeded to strip me of my clothes and make love to me on the divan in the firelight. It was very quick; when he'd finished, he told me I was an incredibly beautiful woman and promptly fell asleep.

I lay there awake, trying to take in what had just happened to me. This was what I had feared for as long as I could remember and now it was finally done. I knew I had turned the most important corner of my life and I was both frightened and exhilarated.

We became lovers. I cleaned his house for him and tried to cook his meals. I pretended to stay at my brother's house but only made a pathetic show of coming in for clothes in the morning before going to work. Will was completely oblivious. Floating on a buoyant cloud of love that made me impulsive, wise, and invincible, I fell completely under Thomas's spell and soon wanted to be with him forever. I thought it was just pure luck that we both worked at the store, and could spend even more time together.

I loved my job at the Monhegan Store. Doug and Harry, the owners, were good to me. I quickly learned how to operate the cash register and keep track of all the accounts. Because most people charged their groceries, I soon learned the names of all the summer and winter people. I also learned that islands tend to be magnets for celebrities, and Monhegan was no exception.

Zero Mostel, known for his acting on Broadway in *Fiddler on the Roof* and his role in *The Producers, A Funny Thing Happened on the Way to the Forum,* and other movies, had a summer home on the island. Most don't know that Zero was also an artist of no small talent and used his island cottage as a studio. During his early acting career during the late forties, Zero was branded a leftist, largely because he ridiculed right wingers during his nightclub comedy shows. MGM, 20th Century Fox, and Columbia all blacklisted him, and this eventually landed him before the House Un-American Activities Committee, where he refused to name names and pled the Fifth.

Zero Mostel (publicity photo)

On Monhegan, Zero was larger than life; he would come booming into the store, making outrageous jokes, befriending everyone, and clowning nonstop. Doug and Harry adored him because he had once hosted them on a visit to New York City, giving them front row tickets to *Fiddler on the Roof.* This was an act of kindness that had thrilled them to no end and Harry wouldn't hesitate to describe to anyone willing to listen how, at one point during the performance, Zero departed from the script to point them out to the audience.

A couple of years later, I saw Zero at an island wedding and we talked for a while about island life. He looked ill and complained of feeling awful because he was trying to lose weight for his upcoming role in *The Merchant* on Broadway. The next day he returned to New York and we got word shortly thereafter that he had collapsed in his dressing room after a rehearsal and died.

Another summer resident, Jamie Wyeth--son of the iconic American painter Andrew Wyeth--was just starting to gain renown as an artist at that time. He and his wife Phyllis had a beautiful cottage overlooking Lobster Cove. I didn't know them well, since they usually had their groceries delivered, but from time to time, the island would be abuzz at the Wyeths' celebrity guests, including Bianca Jagger, Arnold Schwarzenegger, and a myriad of Kennedys, who would yacht over from Hyannis. The parties hosted for these guests at the Wyeth Cottage were reputed to be wild, though this was a social circle I was firmly outside of.

Doug and Harry ran a good store. Doug, the taciturn one, was in charge of meats and cheeses, and Harry, the sweet one, lorded over a first-class wine selection. They had all sorts of strange delicacies on the shelves like canned fiddleheads, black and red caviars, exotic chocolates, canned wild Maine blueberries, and a full line of Pastene Italian foods. Doug and Harry would fill orders dropped off by impatient summer people, and send Thomas out for their delivery, several times a day if necessary.

Their drinking was legendary and sometimes I would show up out of simple kindness to help with the cash register during the evening hours, when I wasn't supposed to be working. Doug could be pretty intimidating at night, reeking of booze, eyes half focused, thrusting change at some frightened tourist, slurring monosyllabic and belligerent replies to any questions asked of him. Harry was pretty much out of it at these times, and just sat behind the counter with a docile and childlike look on his face.

Doug and Harry lived lives that seemed dictated by very strict rules. Doug was the more dominant of the two and would always order Harry about. The most famous saying on Monhegan during that time was, "While you're up Harry," because no matter what Harry was doing—sitting, standing, or lying down taking a nap—Doug would interrupt him with the thinly veiled demand, "While you're up Harry, how 'bout you fix me a drink?"

Doug always piloted the boat when they lobstered, and Harry was always the sternman. On the island, Doug always drove the truck; inshore, Harry always drove their car. While they would bicker endlessly, especially when they got tight, it was generally agreed that Doug and Harry's "marriage" was the most successful on Monhegan.

I really loved those two old guys.

Aside from Dough and Harry, there were many other characters who inhabited Monhegan. The most interesting island summer residents were a group the locals called "Breathers." These were the ethereal followers of a pair of master Gestalt therapists, and their sect of Gestalt practice known as "Sensory Awareness." These Gestalt masters owned half of the old island home called the Influence. This lovely nineteenth-century, square Federal-style building earned its name because a certain island drunkard of bygone days would habitually sleep off his toots under the old house's porch. When his wife would go looking for him, she was told that she could find him "under the Influence."

Breathers got their nickname from the common island assumption that these people were so out of it that they had to be told how to breathe. Every summer they rented the one-room schoolhouse to hold their classes. They wore loose drawstring pants and very mellow attitudes. There they were "reacquainted with their senses;" and for hours each day for the entire summer, they performed very meaningful work on themselves. I became good friends with several Breathers, some of whom seemed to be uncommonly slow finders of their senses since they kept returning to the island faithfully for years for even more lessons. I also noticed that despite all their schooling, some of them had less sense than Jiminy Cricket. But I still enjoyed their unusual and bizarre company. After all, my life wasn't exactly normal, and Breathers were just one more thing that made up the unique fabric of Monhegan.

"The Influence"

Of course, Monhegan wouldn't be complete without its artists. The island was an art colony and everywhere you looked you'd see someone standing behind a portable easel, doing plein air painting as if their life depended on it. Most summer cottages were owned or rented by artists who set up studio hours for obliging tourists to troop on in and buy a painting. Many, besides the Wyeths, were well known at that time, names like Charlie Martin, Ruben Tam, and Zero Mostel. Before them came the great American landscape painters from New York, including George Bellows, Edward Hopper, and Rockwell Kent. The island was steeped in art and locals took the eccentricities of the artists in stride.

Sarah approached me one day and suggested that we take a trip to the mainland to find a clinic and get birth control pills—she was now regularly sleeping with Thomas's best friend and had sense enough to worry about pregnancy. I lacked that sense. When I timidly approached Thomas about the subject, Thomas smiled sadly and kindly explained to me that if I *trusted* him there was no need for me to use birth control. He assured me that everything was going to be fine; I just had to trust him. So, I stayed on the island and trusted. My periods came and went over the summer, so I guess whatever—or whoever—I was trusting did me a good turn.

Life with Thomas was unusual. He'd decided to be a nudist that summer (at home anyway), so anyone who came to call was greeted by a completely naked man. He was very nearsighted, but decided that

145

wearing glasses was bad for his eyesight. He wandered and drove around the island nearly blind as a bat, squinting at everything like a hippie version of Mr. Magoo. He was also very social and had friends visiting constantly to play music and smoke dope.

Sears Gallagher painting on Fish Beach while fisherman cleans fish (Warner Taylor)

Thomas struggled with his guitar, pounding out the same Rolling Stones tunes over and over again, singing in his reedy tenor voice while imagining himself in a rock band. When I was with Thomas I soon understood that my tastes in popular music, running mostly to Elton John and the Eagles, were very childish. I was turned on to the local hippie radio station where I discovered artists like John Prine, Bonnie Raitt, Boz Skaggs, Jerry Jeff Walker, Jackson Browne, Richie Havens, and, of course, the Rolling Stones. Music was the most important expression of art to us in those days and I cultivated myself accordingly.

One day that summer, Thomas got horribly drunk. One of his deliveries was to a notorious island drunkard named Lonnie, who enticed Thomas into his house for a couple of drinks. Two very large and very straight vodkas later, Thomas was weaving the store truck back and forth down the dirt lane until he parked it sideways to its parking spot at the store. Harry stepped out of the store and watched as an extremely inebriated Thomas staggered out of the truck, mumbling about having to get home. He was last seen stumbling down the road toward his house. When I showed up at the Summer Cottage after work I found my nude boyfriend violently heaving his guts up out in the back yard, while a concerned neighbor tried to ply him with Alka-Seltzer. The neighbor, a straitlaced older Jewish man, was doing a very good job of ignoring the fact that Thomas was naked as the day he was born, though I noticed that his equally straitlaced Jewish wife was nowhere to be seen. After this experience Thomas forswore alcohol for the rest of that summer.

Thomas also had some bizarre eating habits. He was a total sweets junkie and would binge on sugary stuff with great regularity. For him to go to the store, buy a half-gallon of chocolate ice cream, and polish the whole thing off in one sitting was not unusual. He would castigate himself endlessly for this lack of character and willpower but the next time the munchies appeared he was right back at the freezer section of the store again. Finally, after one particularly gruesome event involving several dozen sugar donuts, he decided to swear off sugar—which he managed to do for over two years, before succumbing to an unusually attractive wedding cake during a large Monhegan party.

His gut was constantly giving him trouble with what I suspect now was irritable bowel syndrome. He was always complaining about stomach pains and diarrhea and went to doctors for batteries of tests and barium enemas. He finally settled on a special food-combining diet published in a tiny pamphlet available at only the more far-out health food stores. On this diet, he could only eat a couple of different foods at the same time and there were no meat nor animal products allowed. He extolled the wonders of this diet but had to quit it when he lost so much weight he started to look like he was having a hot-and-heavy affair with bulimia.

I learned so much from Thomas—about island life, society, politics, nature, and the ocean. I was like a sponge soaking it all up; while some of it was quite bizarre, it was all enormously interesting, and I felt incredibly proud to be his woman. He had definite opinions about everyone and freely dispensed his wisdom to all. He had summered there all his life so everyone on the island knew him. I was able to become close to Thomas's friends, Tim and Marie, who were real island fishermen with a house of their own. That was how I learned the true inside story of how things worked out there and was drawn even more firmly into the island family that I so craved. For the first time in my life I felt I *belonged*.

Before I showed up that summer, Thomas had avoided having a full-time relationship with any one woman. It was the time of free sex with very little love attached and a different woman would share his bed most nights. He did have one girl on Monhegan, whom I'll call Crystal. Thomas and Crystal had been on-again, off-again for years and she was under the impression that she was the one he would finally hook up with on a permanent basis. She mooned over him constantly before I arrived on the scene, so when I stepped into what she thought was her rightful role, it didn't go over well. I was puzzled for the whole summer as to why this woman would never speak to me or even acknowledge my presence.

Thomas's main goal was to move to Manana and begin a life of independence from the establishment. He had an innate distrust of the real world, with its cops, soldiers, and people of power. His most traumatic experience was a couple of years before, when he'd been thrown in jail in Florida for illegal arms possession. His failure to appear in court after being released on bail made that state off-limits for him.

He'd been living on Monhegan when Ray Phillips, the hermit, died the previous winter, and he had been enlisted to help clean up the shack of health hazards after the old man's body was removed. Thomas's description of removing a half-eaten, partially decomposed sheep carcass from Ray's closet was especially entertaining. For some reason, this experience had a profound effect on Thomas and he became fixated on his desire to live in the hermit's home. While he hinted vaguely about wanting a partner in this venture, usually the issue was skated around and not brought up with any seriousness. He did bring me over to Manana to show me around on our memorable first visit, when I was able to make my acquaintance with Ray Phillips' bathtub. But mostly we were just in love and living our summer romance, one moment at a time.

Hermit shacks on Manana

Summer began to wind down; Sarah went back to California, leaving early with plans to visit family in Colorado on the way. Suddenly, in a complete panic, I realized that I, too, was supposed to go home again. I was only sixteen and would be just starting my third year in high school; it was tricky, but I shyly felt out Thomas about staying. One day he would tell me that school was complete bullshit: I was a woman now and didn't need to go back to the processing plant known as high school, just to be turned out like as a clone of all the other poor mindless souls. The next day he would tell me to go home because I was too young to think about staying with him and I needed to move on. What on earth possessed me to think I could stay?

It was confusing to say the least and a more mature person would have picked up on those giant red flags right then and there. But I was not mature and all I could think about was returning to long bus rides, the restrictive life of a high school student, and my often-depressed mother. The prospects of going home were mind-numbingly awful to me. I didn't want to leave the island and I didn't want to leave Thomas.

Thomas was a great proponent of LSD and had tripped so many times that he'd lost count. He described one trip when he took so much acid that he'd experienced what he called a "white out." This was when the entire universe went white leaving him very much alone. He believed with absolute conviction that all his great wisdom was derived directly from his frequent use of this mind-bending tool and that everyone who sought true awareness should experience it as well. The day before I was to leave we decided to drop acid together. It was my first time, but I had heard Thomas extol the virtues of this marvelous drug so much that I felt ready for it. LSD was going to decide important things about our relationship and help us to determine where our futures lay—in relation to the cosmos as a whole, of course. We swallowed the little LSD-laced pieces of paper with solemn purpose and waited for the trip to arrive.

I have since done acid about three or four times and all the experiences have run together—as they do—so my memories of that first trip are a little hazy. I did not have a bad trip; I've never had a bad trip. I hallucinated and saw things swirling around in true psychedelic fashion. I had incredible insights into the meaning of life that were meaningless, or at least unobtainable during normal states; they would be of no use to me after the trip. I felt love as a tangible thing, but I also saw happiness as a tangible thing, and sadness, and thoughts. All were touchable and held in my hand, all to fade away after it was over— leaving me in wonder and bafflement. It was one hell of an aphrodisiac too, and we screwed until we hurt, but I don't remember attaining any deeper understandings about our relationship, or the cosmos for that matter.

So, the next day Thomas put me on the mail boat and waved goodbye.

I returned to California with a very bad attitude. I was hoping I was pregnant, so I could go back to my Maine lover, which I revealed to my horrified mother. During my absence that summer, Dora, once again deciding a move was in order, had sold our house in Northern California and selected Palm Springs as our new home. I was definitely not pleased to be starting yet another new school.

Palm Springs High, where I started my junior year, was like a surreal scene from the Brady Bunch to me. All the kids wore clean-cut clothes, had spiffy hairdos, and drove nice cars. I couldn't even find anyone to do drugs with. I would sit like a monk alone on the school grounds at lunchtime, eating dates and shunning any contact with my peers. I thought the teachers were all stupid and the things they were teaching infantile. I was absolutely miserable and spent all my time composing long letters to Thomas about how horrible things were. He wrote back equally long letters about how much he missed me. I lost a lot of the weight I had gained from eating all that ice cream with Thomas, and moped.

When my mother made plans to go back to Crescent City to get our belongings, I made plans too. I finally cornered Thomas on the phone and, at a weak moment, got him to ask me to come back. Before he could have second thoughts, I purchased a one-way ticket to Logan Airport in Boston for me and my dog, Alice. I didn't think my mother would like it if I left Alice behind.

Soon after Dora left on her trip up north, I took a cab to the airport and, without a backward glance, flew away. I was sixteen years old and convinced that my life as a child was over.

FLAT ASS CALM

CHAPTER SEVENTEEN ~ FIRST WINTER

Someone's gonna have to explain it to me
I'm not sure what it means.
My baby's feeling funny in the morning,
she's having trouble getting into her jeans...

— *Christopher Charles Lloyd, Marvin Bernard and Jacob Brian*
Dutton

Thomas came the airport to meet me. He looked worried, but I was so happy to see him that I hardly noticed. For some reason, I'd decided we had to go straight out to the Cape to see my father before heading to Maine. I felt it was the right thing to do—introduce my new man to the family and all that. Maybe that's why Thomas was so worried; he was twenty-four to my sixteen and the reality of statutory rape and its various ramifications must have weighed heavily on his mind. But he took me to Truro where my father presided over an interview with his new son-outlaw. Poor Thomas stammered, mumbled, and giggled inappropriately at my father's pointed questions, while I looked worriedly on.

My father took me aside afterwards to tell me that in no uncertain terms (in his opinion) my new partner was mentally unbalanced. He tried very hard to change my mind about my decision to leave home and school, begging me not to "throw my life away." I just shrugged at his foolish, misguided adult ignorance and the next morning Thomas and I left for Maine.

I am still amazed that it was that easy, but I really don't think either of my parents wanted to make a big scene by forcing me to stay. Social mores in the 1970s were also different than they are today, and it was not all that uncommon for teenage girls to leave home and get married. So, they let me go and hoped that I would soon see the error of my ways. Sadly, they'd vastly underestimated my stubbornness.

The next hurdle was a stop at Thomas's family's house in Auburn, Maine, for that inevitable confrontation. Thomas's parents, bless their hearts, were totally confused and terrified about their son's decision to shack up with an underage girl. But they were nothing but kind to me, no matter how exasperated they were with their youngest child. They cajoled, scolded, and pleaded, but we held firm; we were going to the island to spend the winter and that was that. There was nothing they could do.

Soon I was back on Monhegan again, facing the puzzled looks of the islanders, who'd thought I was gone for the winter. We took up residence in the Summer Cottage—an un-winterized cabin perched on the rocks at the water's edge facing the northwest—with the town water shut-off date looming in the near future.

Thomas had been corresponding with the dead hermit's sister, who now owned the Manana shacks we were hoping to occupy, and he requested that we be allowed to live there in exchange for fixing the place up. Unfortunately, she had consulted with a lawyer who advised her not to allow us in the buildings because he was concerned that we could claim squatter's rights. It took the whole winter to convince her lawyer that we could pay rent and not be squatting; he was a little slow on the uptake, or maybe just unwilling to lose the consultation fees.

We immediately contracted a case of head lice. Thomas had loaned the house to a hippie friend who'd used our bed and left the little loathsome critters behind for us to pick up. Thomas assured me the simple home remedy of immersing one's head in kerosene could eliminate them. I watched with horror as he proceeded to fill a basin with lamp oil and lower his head into it. This was not the prissy, unscented oil you can now buy in pretty bottles in department stores. This was plain old thick, oily, nasty, stinky, yellow kerosene and there was no way I would consent to immersing my blonde tresses in it. Thomas, who had never actually *tried* this remedy before, soon regretted his rash action because it took days to wash the stuff out and it didn't kill the lice to boot. We ended up getting some good old-fashioned RID at an inshore drugstore. That took care of the problem.

George Bellows (1882-1925) "Harbor at Monhegan" 1913

It wasn't long before we started to learn more about each other, not surprisingly finding that we both shared a very dysfunctional past. Strangely enough, it was drugs—namely LSD—that peeled away our protective layers to expose our fragile and vulnerable insides to each other. Our second trip down LSD lane together occurred shortly after my return to the east coast, while Thomas and I were visiting some old friends of his outside of Boston. These friends, two men and one woman, whose relationship was an honest-to-God ménage à trois, offered us a place to stay and some serious recreational drugs. We happily accepted both offers, settled ourselves in the spare bedroom, and dropped our acid.

While we were tripping that night, I recounted my entire childhood to Thomas, starting from when I first fell in love with Monhegan, through my parent's divorce, up to when I returned to the island. While Thomas watched, mesmerized, my voice and vocabulary reverted back to the high-pitched tone of a ten-year-old and, as my tale progressed, my affect matured into the person I was at that time.

It was also during this trip that Thomas described the crushing depressions he'd suffered during his teenage years and early adulthood. He described in great detail desolate scenes of himself sitting for long periods of time with the barrel of a gun in his mouth, trying to draw up the courage to pull the trigger. This he blamed on his oppressive upbringing in a small Maine city during the 1950s and 60s and a mother who (he claimed) stopped loving him and his siblings when she went back to work when Thomas was ten.

When Thomas was very young, his older brother picked on him mercilessly and his parents didn't do much to stop it. His brother would hold him down and spit in his face or find other creative ways to humiliate him, until Thomas was finally old enough to defend himself. This childhood abuse had a somewhat paradoxical effect on Thomas and he became a passive youth who didn't want to leave home. When he dropped out of college during his first year, unable to deal with life's smallest obstacles, his parents sent him to a psychologist in the frantic hope of fixing their troubled son.

I would often curse this psychologist later because Thomas was able to discover and express his anger through therapy, but did not continue any further in his treatment to find out how to deal appropriately with it. The trips to the shrink entitled Thomas to a 4-F exemption from the draft, and he was able to declare himself "well" after only a year of therapy, having discovered that liberal doses of marijuana, LSD, and sex were all he needed to keep his demons at bay. He smugly informed me that he'd figured the shrink's methods out and knew all the answers, so further therapy was unnecessary.

It was late October and the cottage was getting chilly. During a gale, large waves that had been built by cold Canadian northwesterly winds would throw seawater against the house with a loud smack! We slept in a room in the back away from the water to try to stay a little warmer. It was in this bedroom in early November that I knew the moment I became pregnant. After we made love, I suddenly had a brief vision of a little blond-haired boy and I knew with absolute certainty that I was going to have a baby.

Soon after this strange occurrence, I had my first meeting with the "other" Thomas. I truly don't remember what I said, but it started out with us just sitting on the bed together. Maybe he caught me in a little white lie, or I made some thoughtless teasing comment about some cute guy on the island, but the next thing I knew I was in the direct path of a rage the likes of which I had not seen before. Thomas turned white with fury and told me that I was the lowest piece of shit he had ever known. With deadly calm, dripping hate in every syllable, my lover informed me that he did not love me anymore; I was a worthless, lying, immature bitch, and I was to leave the island immediately, never to return. I could feel the blood drain out of my body, leaving me completely weak and limp. Before I even had a chance to dwell in my self-pity, he screamed at me to leave the fucking house NOW!

Somehow, I managed to stumble out the door into the brilliant autumn sunshine. I walked for hours in a daze, while I tried to make sense of what had just happened. What had I done? How could I make it better? Did I really have to leave? I didn't WANT to leave. Oh God what was I going to DO? I had very little money; most of my summer savings had gone toward my plane ticket. I was so in love with Thomas and I was pretty sure I was pregnant. There was no one I could talk to or confide in. I was completely alone. I must have presented an odd sight on the island that day, wandering aimlessly up and down the short dirt roads with no place to go, tears streaming down my face. But the islanders didn't appear to notice and left me alone in my grief.

Thomas tracked me down later in the afternoon. He grudgingly allowed that maybe we could work things out and he was now willing to forgive me. I immediately felt overwhelming joy flooding in where only despair had existed such a short time before. We made love with great passion that night and he told me that I was beautiful, his true soulmate. I convinced myself that his earlier anger was just an aberrant blip on the screen and I firmly believed that the best thing to do was just forget about it as soon as possible.

I cannot tell you how many times this scene repeated. I just know that it was a regular part of my life with this man for the next six years.

I soon found that things were either going fairly well or horribly wrong. It all depended on the mood swings that were dictating Thomas's behavior like a master puppeteer. One day would be happy; we'd get high together, laugh, and he'd tell me he loved me over and over again, but the next day I'd be confronted by a terrifying monster of such despair and hatred that I would quake in fear. It was a constant game of hide-and-seek with Thomas's demons.

I recently discussed this pattern with my current husband who, like most people, had a hard time understanding why I didn't just walk away. "Why on earth did you stay? Couldn't you see what was happening?"

The simple answer is no, I couldn't see what was happening. It was right in front of my nose and even when it reached out and literally smacked me, I still couldn't see it. I had loved people whose behavior was insane since I was a little girl who watched her bare-bottomed mother run out of the house into the night. I was terribly afraid to go back to my old life, which also sucked, and my pride and stubbornness just wouldn't let me admit I was wrong.

The Summer Cottage became even more inhospitable, so Thomas found us a little bunkhouse to live in for the winter. We could stay there free in exchange for insulating it. There was no running water, but the well was just across the street; of course, there was no electricity. Monhegan had no central power in those days and only those with generators were able to enjoy all those fancy electrical conveniences. LP gas was the staple source of energy for stoves, hot water heaters, refrigerators, and lighting. Thomas's friends, Tim and Marie, had installed a windmill to generate power at their new home, but the thing blew to pieces during the first big blow. Monhegan's winds were just too gusty and erratic for that particular form of alternative energy. Later solar panels would sprout up on many roofs, providing many with DC power for lights, water pumps, and other uses.

The only telephone service was via a somewhat precarious cable snaked across over ten miles of sea bottom to the mainland, prone to breaking and long periods of uselessness. If a phone call was to be made, we would have to go down to the store or to one of the inns to use the old operator-assisted payphones.

Monhegan Lobsterman (Penobscot Marine Museum)

The locals would leave their CB radios on all the time, using them to chat with each other and eavesdrop on interesting conversations (CBs were eventually phased out in favor of more marine-oriented VHF radios). This form of communication could provide hours of entertainment. The most memorable exchange that took place on the CB radio involved an irate wife who was trying to get her inebriated husband to leave the fish house—where all the men would congregate and drink themselves silly each night—and return home for supper. When she said with dead seriousness, "Samuel, if you don't come home *right now*, the next thing you are going to hear is the sound of your guitar being smashed," she had everyone's undivided attention. Sure enough, the radio's next emission was the crunching, splintering, screeching sound of a fine piece of musical woodwork being hit forcibly with a hammer, over and over again.

And of course, there was the oft-repeated exchange between Winnie and Vernon, an older couple who were still besotted with each other after thirty years of marriage. At lunchtime Winnie would call up Vernon out on his boat, to find out if he'd partaken of the lunch she packed for him, and she never failed to ask,

"Vernon, have you et yer pickle yet?"

This became a common, if baffling, Monhegan greeting: "Have you et yer pickle yet?"

I was thrilled to be spending a winter on the island, something that only the hardiest of souls attempted. It quickly became apparent that neither of us had very much money, though. Our savings from working at the store were very low and the only work Thomas would do on the island was scuba diving on lobster boats and moorings—something that was occasional at best. He did not want to be a sternman that winter, this being a hard job that required obeying a boat captain; something that was to be avoided at all cost.

It wasn't long before Thomas figured that the best way for us to get some good hard cash and maintain our sense of dignity was by dealing in largish quantities of marijuana. He had spent a couple of winters in Tucson, Arizona, and had made some connections there, so before I knew it, we were boarding a Greyhound bus together in Portland and heading west.

It took three days to get to Tucson. The bus was boring and cramped, and Thomas blew up at me before we reached Philadelphia over some trivial issue that I have no recollection of. Hurt and angry, I retreated off the bus at the Philly terminal and wandered around the station for as long as I could before departure time. When I returned I saw Thomas disembarking from the bus, but when he saw me he quickly got back on. He had finally decided that I wasn't coming back and had come to look for me. I was able to take a tiny bit of satisfaction in knowing that I had him worried, for a moment anyway. We spent most of the rest of the trip in stony silence until he finally thawed enough to forgive me.

When we got to Tucson, tired and incredibly dirty, he took me to a laundromat to use the bathroom and wash up. During my turn in the bathroom I forgot to lock the door and the manager walked in on me

160

while I was standing in front of the sink completely bare-assed. Thomas berated me for hours afterwards for being so stupid and allowing that man to see me. By now I had learned that there was no sense in arguing. I kept my mouth shut and prayed that his anger would just go away. Usually it did.

We met up with the contact: a guy Thomas had worked for in the past who smuggled pot in from Mexico in his spare time. He took us to his apartment and casually pulled a couple of kilos of grass out of a large walk-in closet that appeared to have about a ton of the stuff stashed inside. He left us there and we hung out until it was time to catch the bus home. The marijuana was hidden in my canvas suitcase and checked through with our bags in the bottom of the Greyhound bus. We sweated bullets but we, and our illicit load, finally arrived safely back in Maine.

Later we found out that the day after we left Tucson, the drug dealer's apartment was raided by the DEA and he was thrown in jail. He, of course, thought we had ratted him out. I suppose it was only the luck of beginners or fools that kept us safe, and sometimes, during a bad moment, I can still envision myself in a Tucson jail, a pregnant, clueless sixteen-year-old pot trafficker.

Dealing that marijuana carried us through the winter. Periodically we would take trips to the mainland and sell nickel and dime bags to various potheads we knew for a ridiculous profit. Thomas would put on his special dope-dealing outfit—black-mirrored glasses, black turtleneck jersey, and black jeans—and we would visit his more disreputable friends who held special parties to distribute the stuff... kind of like a freak's version of a Tupperware party. Thomas was always really jittery and nervous during these encounters and he would make lots of trips to the bathroom before and after our little jaunts.

Some of the dope proceeds bought us an old VW bus to use on our inshore trips. I had gotten my license the day I'd turned sixteen in California, so I was able to pilot our new chariot and learn the tricky art of winter driving. It had no heat, and we froze our asses off in it all winter, but that old bus got us around. The defroster didn't work either and if there was any freezing rain we were completely unable to see out the windshield. Once I had to stop every hundred yards or so and scrape vigorously at an inch of accumulated ice in order to see enough to go another hundred yards down the road. One time, when we were stopped at an intersection, the bus mysteriously stopped running. What we didn't know at the time was that the fuel line had come loose and sprayed gasoline all over the motor in the back of the bus. Thomas turned the key, and immediately there was a loud "BOOM!" that blew the cover off the engine compartment, right onto the hood of a car that had pulled up behind us. The resultant fire burned all the wires and hoses, but we soon got it repaired and were back on the road again.

For meat that winter, Thomas decided we would take a deer. The island was teeming with them and the island residents, in an attempt to keep the herd down, vigorously hunted them each fall. Deer were not indigenous to Monhegan. A couple of islanders had brought a few out during the fifties with the intention of hosting fall hunting parties as a money-making scheme; the animals had proliferated like mad. The state of Maine did not oversee Monhegan's deer harvest and no licenses were required to take them. As a result, several families would take numerous deer each winter to stock their freezers with venison. There was never any follow-through on the hunting party idea, nor were any flower or vegetable gardens on the island safe from the deer's capricious foraging. Monheganers erected many ingenious fencing devices in a vain attempt to keep them out, but it wasn't until the Lyme disease scare of the late 1990s, when hired sharpshooters killed off all the deer, that an island daylily dared to bloom again.

One gray fall day Thomas set out with his father's old WWII Russian Army rifle and quickly shot a big doe. Thomas had a great love of guns. Prior to his Florida arrest he would travel with a sawed-off shotgun under the seat of his car. He'd collected several weapons and was probably the world's only hippie NRA wannabe. He was sure that the current political regime was plotting to take away our arms and the only way to be truly prepared was by being hugely fortified and loaded for bear at all times. He taught me how to shoot his rifle and shotgun and, with my earlier BB gun experience still fresh in my mind, I was fully prepared for when the mother-raper government bastards finally came to take our homes and children away.

After killing the deer, Thomas borrowed a truck, brought the carcass home, and deposited it at my feet. This was my first experience with a truly large dead animal and I really had no idea how I would react. All my vegetarianism went out the window as Thomas's great passion for teaching won out the day and I quickly became fascinated by the anatomy of the animal. Soon I was examining each organ with interest and learning about various cuts of meat. We hung the deer in the living room of the Summer Cottage and, while it dripped slowly onto the newspapers we'd placed under it, I helped Thomas remove the skin and guts and chop all the various parts up into small pieces for freezing. Soon we had that living, breathing creature reduced to packages of chops, loin, and hamburger. To preserve the meat, we simply turned the old Servel gas refrigerator at the cottage down to its lowest setting and—while it wasn't exactly a deep freeze—it froze the venison enough to keep it for the winter, though it did taste a tad gamy by spring.

Our diet that year consisted mostly of deer meat, brown rice, omelets, and bulk cheese we got at the island food co-op. Vegetables were few and far between and I was often the first one at the store on boat days, jockeying for a chance at the rare head of lettuce or broccoli that would trickle out to our island. Sometimes all the bananas would freeze on the mail boat trip, so I would get them for nothing and make lots of banana bread.

We had acquired a couple of kittens, two fluffy black Maine Coon cats with white noses. Thomas named them Mewie and Pewie. He insisted on not having them fixed, thinking his explanation that they "weren't broken" was very witty. The cats learned quickly to avoid him because he fell into the habit of kicking them when they got in the way. One day, however, Pewie was too slow and Thomas's kick broke his front leg, entailing a visit to the vet on the mainland for an x-ray and a splint. Later Mewie went off to live with another more hospitable island family and Pewie stayed with us, later to become what was likely the world's only cat with a vasectomy. Thomas found a vet willing to tie the kitty's tubes instead of performing the usual castration so that our tomcat could continue to enjoy his sex life, this being of great importance to Thomas.

After two missed periods, I told Thomas I was pregnant and he was gratifyingly pleased and excited. He had proud images of himself as a father and was very anxious to assume this new role. He babied me nonstop, even bringing me breakfast in bed on occasion. Our friend Marie was astonished when she came by for a visit early one Valentine's Day and found me propped up in bed consuming an enormous heart-shaped chocolate cake. Thomas had baked it himself and presented it to me as a surprise that morning. Marie didn't know I was pregnant and she went away that day thinking I was the most spoiled rotten girlfriend Thomas had ever had.

The nature of Thomas's and my relationship changed in a big way during the early months of my pregnancy; I stopped wanting to have sex with him. It all started as a result of my morning sickness. One morning he made the usual overtures and I turned away from him. I could feel nothing but nausea, and sex was the last thing I wanted just then. In his usual overblown fashion, Thomas was hurt, offended, and outraged that I'd refused him. I tried to explain that I felt sick, but he became angry and insisted that I didn't love him anymore or find him attractive. After this followed a lot of sulking on his part and something changed within me from that day on. To my great chagrin, I just never really wanted to make love to him anymore. I always had to be pushed, cajoled, and pleaded with to have sex. I was sure there was something dreadfully wrong with me; I actually enjoyed sex and I really loved the intimacy, but I didn't want to have sex with my partner and I couldn't figure out why. My desire for him was completely shut off and would stay that way for the rest of our time together. Every night I would pray that he wouldn't ask for it and almost every night he did. I think he looked upon it as a challenge to get me to bend to his will and it was only with great reluctance that I always complied.

My belly grew, my breasts softened and expanded with stretch marks decorating their sides. I only had the vaguest idea of what was going on in respect to childbearing and child rearing. I was the youngest of all my parents' children, so I had no experience with babies. I didn't even *like* babies. I knew with supreme confidence that I would love my baby though.

It would all work out somehow.

We kept my pregnancy secret. Thomas had definite ideas about birth and delivery that were unlikely to be shared by most people. His dream was for me to have the baby on Manana in our newly fixed-up hermit shack with a midwife in attendance and himself catching the little bundle when it emerged. This baby would be something that was truly his and Thomas had many ideas on how to form it into the perfect little human being. He was reluctant for me to have prenatal care and was adamant that if I did see a doctor it had to be a woman. He informed me that all male OB-GYNs were perverts who loved to play with women's private parts and he was not going to allow it. Unfortunately, as there were no female obstetricians in the area, my prenatal care was nonexistent. I was young and healthy, thank goodness, and nothing went wrong with me. The gods were smiling on me because I was repulsed by alcohol and pot during both of my pregnancies and was thus able to spare my children the devastating effects of those substances during their incubation.

Monhegan winter scene (Lorimer Brackett)

That first winter I found there were many other important facts I had to learn while living with Thomas. He believed that all women were essentially whores at heart and that the victim of a rape usually deserved it. I was instructed that only prostitutes shaved their legs and armpits, so I had to refrain from that practice. Obviously, bras were not acceptable attire for a lady, nor (for some strange reason) were underpants (I defied that directive). I also learned that all men looked upon women merely as conquests and that sex was the overriding factor in any male-female relationship. I had to use extreme caution in how I interacted with other men; I found out very quickly that Thomas's jealousies would erupt in a toxic rage at the slightest provocation.

The fact that I was a virgin when Thomas first seduced me was, for him, the most important factor in our relationship. During his worked-up states, he often would convince himself that I was not really a virgin when we met, and he was constantly accusing me of having had sex with another man before or after our first get-together. He was convinced that I always desired sex with some other man and was scheming ways of cheating on him.

I had to represent the woman inviolate, a pure vessel that had not been tainted in any way. This was a hard order to fill; my immaturity, fear, and desire to please would at times compel me to manufacture a past for myself that did not include any contact with any persons of the opposite sex, not even kissing my first boyfriend when I was fourteen. Thomas was intent in ferreting out my falsehoods and he was always grilling me about my past. Inevitably I found myself getting tripped up by the lies I constructed to try to protect myself—the end result being more rages, recriminations, and temporary expulsions from his life as punishment for my dishonesty. During one of these rages, when I was about four months pregnant, he went as far as to demand that I leave the island on the next boat and get an abortion, that we were FINISHED (of course he "forgave" me later).

Thomas claimed to hate liars more than anything; unfortunately, I was a liar. My ingrained childhood habit of dishonesty had finally come back to bite me in the ass.

CHAPTER EIGHTEEN ~ ISLAND LIFE

I would never belong to a group that would
accept someone like me as a member.

—Groucho Marx

As a certified marine diver, Thomas would occasionally get jobs diving on the propeller of a lobster boat to cut away the rope (known as warp) that would periodically tangle there. On Monhegan, it was far more efficient for the fishermen to hire a scuba diver when they got "wound up" than take a whole day to go to the mainland and get hauled out. Due to the unpredictable weather, very few would beach their boats on the island beaches during a tide, so the demand for a diver was pretty high during lobstering season.

The job included removing pot warp from the propeller, inspecting the mooring chains, and checking the zincs. Mindful of the salt water electrolysis that eats away at metal, fishermen would attach small blocks of zinc to the hulls of their boats, so that the zincs—not the precious propeller, shaft, or boat fastenings—would be eaten away first. When the zincs were worn down sufficiently, they had to be replaced.

Diving was a miserable job, but Thomas took a perverse macho pleasure in it. He had a wetsuit that only partially kept out the cold, so he would try frantically to get the lines cut on the propeller shaft before he succumbed to hypothermia. Fortunately, our friends Tim and Marie had built a new house on the island, complete with hot running water; we would bolt down there for showers on a regular basis.

Marie was likely the first woman on the island to work on a lobster boat as a sternman with her lobsterman husband. At that time women were considered bad luck on a boat, as was the color blue. It was with great consternation that the older islanders watched the wave of young hippies take up residence on the island in the late 1960s and early 70s, then proceed to turn the carefully constructed island world upside down. These mostly former summer kids moved to Monhegan in order to leave the establishment, dodge the war, learn lobstering, and break all the rules.

Marsden Hartley (1877-1943) "Lobster Fishermen" 1940-41

One old lobsterman took Tim law aside one day and carefully explained to him how women were to be treated. Women were supposed to stay home, keep house, and prepare meals for the men. Many of the island wives didn't even have a driver's license and their trips to the mainland, done only in the company of their husbands, were few and very restricted. It was considered indecent to see these young girls bagging bait in the fish house and standing in the stern of a lobster boat.

But things were changing. I did notice that while the newer attitudes allowed the women to bag bait and work in the stern of the boat, it wasn't until many years later that there was an actual lobsterwoman on the island who had a *male* sternman. She painted her boat blue, which might have been a statement as well.

Once the taboo of women on the boat was broken, young women would apply for the job of sternmen, often getting the job with lobstermen who were married to traditional stay-at-home island wives. Then the stories would circulate about how so-and-so's boat had been seen sitting idle in the water off the backside of the island in the middle of the day for an hour without anyone on deck. This infuriated the island wives and made me wonder if it was the *wives* who had originally decreed that women on boats were bad luck.

Monhegan's lobster fleet was one of the most prosperous in the state. This was due to some pretty canny foresight on the part of the lobstermen many years before, when the island community took it upon itself to protect their fishing grounds. They did this by getting the State of Maine to legislate that the season in which lobsters could be harvested within a two-mile boundary around the island would be open only from January first through the end of May. This effectively excluded the mainland fishermen fishing the Monhegan waters and summer visitors from setting a few traps, and took full advantage of the fact that the deep waters around the island were prime winter fishing grounds. Lobsters migrate to greater depths during cold weather and—due to their scarcity in the winter—the price goes up accordingly. The downside of all this was that lobstering took place during the winter, the most inhospitable time of year to be on a boat doing what was hard and dangerous work at the best of times.

Monhegan's harbor was only semi-sheltered, and sat wide open to the southerly seas. The best place to launch a skiff to get out to a boat in the harbor was off Fish Beach. A small breakwater of tumbled rocks had been constructed at the south end of the beach to help divert the worst of the seas from that direction, but it was often a bad place to try to get a boat in the water.

While it is hard to imagine a lobsterman cooperating with anyone—they are the true cowboys of the ocean—the men of Monhegan did try to work together. Someone at the fish house always kept an eye

169

on the harbor for the last straggler after an exhausting day's work. It was by mutual unspoken agreement that during rough weather they waited while each skiff rode a wave onto the beach, coming forward to lend a hand hauling it and its occupants out of the reach of the next roller.

George Bellows (1882-1925) "The Big Dory" 1913

"Trap Day" was the long-awaited first day of the year when all the gear could finally be put into the water to begin catching lobsters and bringing in the big bucks. So as not to give an unfair advantage to anyone getting out first to the best spots, the fishermen tried to wait until everyone was ready before getting started. Trap Day was the time of year when tempers and emotions ran high, the time when everyone's livelihood depended on the thin thread of equipment working as it should and everyone staying healthy.

The preferred place to load up the boats with traps was off the wharf, and each fisherman staked out a spot a day or two before the big day to stack his traps. In those days lobster pots were made of oak, weighted with slabs of cement so they'd sink, and far heavier than the wire traps we see today. They would be piled six or more high on the wharf, with just enough space to back a truck between the towering piles. Little alleyways would separate each owner's traps and the wharf soon was transformed into an alien cityscape with rickety wooden skyscrapers looming ten feet or higher up to the sky.

This was a time of big employment on the island. Sternmen were hired—sometimes for a percentage of the catch, but usually for a flat daily rate—and temporary helpers were procured for the week or so it took to get everything in the water. Of course, Thomas and I took part that year, working for Tim and Marie, helping them load the lobstering gear onto their old wooden boat. They'd bought their boat from a retiring lobsterman a few years before and changed the name to better suit them. (Changing the name of a boat was also considered very bad luck.)

The harbor was filled with boats and lobster cars: very large wooden crates, ten feet long, five feet wide, and three feet deep, with hinged doors on the top. The cars were attached to moorings during the fishing season to hold the lobster catch until it could be sold. Each lobsterman had his own car and periodically they would "bail" out the lobsters, either taking them to the mainland to sell or to a boat called a lobster smack that came out to the island to buy up the catch. Some of the nosier island wives would watch with binoculars while the bailing was taking place to try to ascertain how many lobsters their husband's competitors had procured.

Before the season began, bait, in the form of fresh herring, was bought in bulk from a visiting seine boat. It was then heavily salted to preserve it for the season and stored in large bins in the fish houses, later to be bagged in small net bags, each to be placed in a trap when it was set overboard. The fish houses were shared in an almost communal fashion, the space within divided up and rented for a pittance to the younger, newer fishermen by the old-time fishermen whose families had owned the buildings for generations. It was a good idea to be on good terms with the guy whose fish house you were using, or you could find yourself in the unenviable position of trying to find another fish house to store your bait.

The members of the fishing community got along with each other, but it was often an uneasy alliance. The temptation to criticize a lazier fisherman or point out another's shortcomings behind his back was never passed up. By definition, lobstermen were all colorful individuals and Monhegan had a full spectrum. There were the really gung-ho guys who got up at the crack of dawn and were the last ones in at night. They had the nicest boats, and everything was spic-and-span. Then there were the ho-hum fishermen who set only a few traps, had boats that were ill cared for, and only fished once a week or so. Everyone was tolerated, and everyone was judged. It was the island way.

Fish Beach (Penobscot Marine Museum)

Tim and Marie were among the better fishermen, making unheard of (to me) sums of money each year and working hard. They came home exhausted each day and had several drinks to relax. Often when Thomas and I showed up on a day they didn't go out, Marie would be nursing a big hangover with a beer for breakfast, an old remedy known as the hair of the dog that bit you.

Tim and Marie's house was our haven. We would go let ourselves in every other day to use the shower and (if they were out fishing) raid their refrigerator like little children. The house was new and light and warm and, while we never admitted it, our salvation from a life of complete squalor in our dank and tiny bunkhouse. How they put up with us, I don't know, although Marie did finally ask us to stop eating all their food once, which made me feel very ashamed. Thomas and I were like refugees who needed someone to take care of us. I was grateful for their good heartedness and willingness to take us in. We were able to pretend we were roughing it while having all the comforts of home just a five-minute walk away.

Winter passed slowly, and we spent a lot of time hanging out in our little bunkhouse because it was usually too cold or stormy to go outside. I was amazed by the extremes of weather that winter. Monhegan was a place of opposites and intense contrasts; summer was idyllic: sunny seas, gentle breezes, green grasses and beautiful wildflowers. Winter transformed it into a place of blinding gales, freezing spray, and crashing waves. The ground froze hard and the predominant color was gray; a steely ocean under lowering skies, dreary weathered houses withstanding yet another year of abuse from the elements.

Sea Smoke (U.S. Navy Photo)

When the temperature dropped into the single digits the ocean would start to release vapor, long wispy tendrils of fog that emanated from the water's surface reaching for the sky like bony fingers. The vapor, or "sea smoke" would envelop the boats in the harbor. Then, creeping stealthily onto the island, it would coat everything with a sugar-like layer of ice. Snow would come of course, but Monhegan's snows were of an elusive and wayward nature. Snowstorms were almost always accompanied by wind and the wind would blow most of it off the island before it could stick. We did have some mighty drifts though, often many feet high, while the ground would be completely bare just a couple of yards away.

Ice was the more predominant nuisance, since the tempering effect of the ocean would warm up a big snowstorm to the point where it would turn to rain on the island. Accumulated snow would turn to slush, then freeze. Winter residents of Monhegan all had a characteristic walk, a peculiar waddle necessary to get you down the road that had several inches of ice on it... without falling and breaking your ass. The road commissioner's main job each winter was distributing beach sand with a shovel out of the back of a pickup truck onto the roads, just so folks could get around.

We would bundle up during a bad storm and battle our way across the island to the backside to watch huge waves climb up the side of Whitehead, a cliff well over one hundred feet tall. Gull Rock, its promontory sixty feet high, would frequently be completely enveloped with blue water. There was simply nothing between Portugal and us to stop the waves. During a particularly massive storm, the ocean would build and build until it crashed into our tiny island, in an ultimately fruitless attempt to annihilate us all. Monhegan was always able to withstand these onslaughts, but the tiny frail structures built by men over the centuries often fell prey to the relentless sea.

It was during that winter that we had a particularly bad storm, known as the Groundhog Day gale of 1976. It was a big blow from the southeast, which is a very bad direction for Monhegan to have to endure a squall. Her harbor was wide open in the southerly direction, and the boats moored there were vulnerable; a fisherman's greatest fear is losing his boat.

The waves built to enormous heights and rolled up Fish Beach, damaging the old fish houses that had stood there for two hundred years. Tim and Marie's lobster car tore loose from its mooring in the harbor and sailed out of the gut by Smutty Nose, finally to crash on the rocks at Deadman's Cove; they lost every lobster they'd caught since Trap Day. Fortunately, no boats were lost but there was a lot of cleaning up to do afterwards. The wharf had taken quite a beating, losing much of its fill and requiring major repairs the following summer.

Thomas and I took frequent trips to the mainland—as much as our toes could stand, that is. The *Laura B* was the mail boat. She was a beamy old former Army T boat constructed out of wood back in the forties—about fifty feet long and built like a nautical version of the

174

proverbial brick shithouse. Owned and captained at the time by "Young Earl," who had taken over from his father "Old Earl" many years before, she regularly made the eleven-mile trip back and forth from Port Clyde to Monhegan, often during weather that would make a whale sick. Back in the stern, where the passengers were supposed to sit, there was no heat; therefore, the hour-long trip was a constant battle against frostbite.

Winslow Homer (1836-1910) "Watching a Breaker – A High Sea" 1896

During a particularly nasty gale, the *Laura B* would be canted almost sideways as she fought her way over the towering waves, bucking and heaving, throwing the unfortunate passengers in the stern around like marbles in a can. Sometimes the old adage, "Tie her to the mast!" was followed quite literally because the only way to avoid certain injury or concussion was by literally tying yourself to something. The stern was boarded up with sheets of plywood over the windows and it was a pretty gloomy and depressing place to be stuck for the seventy minutes it usually took to get inshore.

The mail boat did not run if the weather was so bad that a landing at Monhegan's wharf was inadvisable. The post office, being the information center on the island at the time, would be inundated with worried passengers-to-be on a rough day; all of them waiting for the verdict of whether there would be a boat. Some greeted the cancellations with annoyance, but most breathed a sigh of relief. There was something absolute and final about being stuck on an island with absolutely no way off. Doctors and dentists inshore were accustomed to last-minute appointment breaking and would usually make accommodations to islanders. If someone had to catch a flight or had some other very important engagement, they were wise to leave the island several days in advance to be sure. The boat almost always ran the day following a cancellation unless there was a really huge storm that lasted several days.

Al Melenbacker (1920-2014) "Laura B" (Private collection)

Old Monhegan joke: Approach a nervous newcomer on the Monhegan wharf while he or she is trying to summon up the courage to get on board the *Laura B* during a particularly nasty day. The old boat is bucking and heaving at her lines with great groaning and crunching noises as she bangs against the pilings. Casually ask if they want to know what happened to the *Laura A.*

The mail boat crew consisted of a couple of derelict old men: one a murderer recently released from Thomaston, Maine's maximum-security prison, and Junior. Junior was a big, square-shaped, bullet-headed guy with the small eyes characteristic of fetal alcohol syndrome. He also boasted the intellect of a gnat. Junior was hired for his strength; he could heave a refrigerator around without even breaking a sweat. Sometime during his thirties Junior decided it was time to get himself a wife, and he would pursue the single island girls mercilessly around the wharf during the summertime. While he never actually caught any, islanders assumed that if he were successful, he would drag her by her hair to his cave to have his way with her.

I used to fear Junior with great conviction during my unattached days because he had his eye on me for a while, but once I was officially taken, he left me alone. Junior's favorite way to amuse himself was by appearing in the stern of the *Laura B* during a really horrendous trip. There he would proceed to open a very smelly can of sardines in tomato sauce and consume them in a particularly Junior-like fashion in front of the queasy passengers, with the oil and partially masticated tomato-fish sludge dribbling down his chin. There was always a rush for the rail during these performances. He was quite a piece of work, that Junior.

When we finally arrived inshore, a car buried in snow with a dead battery often greeted us. You learned very quickly never to set your emergency brake when you parked to go to the island because it would be frozen in place when you returned, and wouldn't release without major help. If and when the old bus started, it would be another two hours of freezing in the unheated VW as we slipped and fishtailed to Auburn toward the sanctuary of a big warm house with TV, washer, dryer, and parents who took us in with open arms.

Thomas's parents became my own. We spent all our holidays there and I found the predictability of turkey and mince pie at Thanksgiving and turkey and Swedish butter cookies at Christmas to be very soothing. His mother was starting to slide into undiagnosed early-onset Alzheimer's disease and her constant repeating of questions caused us much bafflement and—for Thomas—much annoyance. His father was a sweet, gentle man who never had a harsh word to say. Their house, where Thomas grew up, was a big Maine farmhouse with an attached carriage house where Thomas's father indulged his habit of not throwing things away, much to his wife's disgust. It was a home for me where Thomas rarely dared to treat me poorly and where I could be assured of affection and getting all my clothes clean.

Thomas's paternal grandmother had traveled the world and brought back many strange pieces of furniture from the Far East. The guestroom bed was a Chinese affair built like a little red-lacquered room with intricately carved walls, entranceway, and poles for the fabric hangings that weren't there. That is where we slept, and I was fascinated by it; I would also stare for hours at the little jade figures in the glass cases that ornamented the room like a museum. This grandmother was also a great patron of the arts and while summering on Monhegan bought many paintings from the artists who congregated there. These works graced all the walls of their house and the island summer cottage—most quite good and some quite valuable. I grew to love that home and felt safe there as nowhere else.

CHAPTER NINETEEN ~ ORCA

You need chaos in your soul to give birth to a dancing star.

—Nietzsche

S ummer arrived, and we finally got permission to move to Manana. We immediately set to work getting our home on the little island ready for the baby and us. My bulging belly had become apparent to everyone and—when asked—we acknowledged that there was a child on the way. We were purposely vague about its due date, though. I had an instinctual idea what day the baby would be born and what his sex would be, but we didn't want the nosy island folks to start urging me inshore at the time of its imminent arrival. So, we pretended the baby was due a month later. We placed an ad in the *Maine Times* for a midwife to come to the island and attend the birthing. Soon a woman from central Maine answered us, stating that she loved the idea of an island vacation while doing her job.

We ordered and devoured books on birthing; Frederick LeBoyer on babies coming into the world underwater, the La Leche League on breastfeeding and natural birth control, Lamaze on natural childbirth. There were also lots of books on how the male-dominated American Medical Association was trying to take away a woman's right to control the birth of her child and how safe and wonderful home births were. It was all terribly abstract to me, but I dutifully read everything, practiced the breathing exercises, and figured I was prepared for the great event.

Alice Kent Stoddard (1884-1976) "Monhegan Island Harbor Looking Toward Manana" 1910

I got bigger and bigger and the climb up the side of Manana became more and more arduous. I must have presented quite a spectacle climbing in and out of the skiff on my way back and forth across the harbor, scrambling over the seaweed-covered rocks in my gravid state. There was a lot of whispering and our friend Marie relayed much of it to us. Finally, when our midwife showed up, Marie asked us point blank if indeed we planned to have that baby on Manana, where no child had been born in recorded history.

I began to worry. Maybe this wasn't such a good idea, maybe we should reconsider... Our midwife took one look at our little shack and agreed that it might be better to have the baby on the bigger island after all. So, we moved over to the Summer Cottage and waited there… and waited and waited. I lost my mucus plug and still nothing happened.

The midwife turned out to be an incessant talker. She had her spoiled and obnoxious child with her, constantly whining for attention. They were both getting on our nerves. I thought, well maybe we should try going to the mainland, you know, *just in case*… so we took the mail boat ashore and went to Thomas's parents' other summer cottage in the small coastal village of Muscongus. We waited some more, but there was no sign of anything going on down below.

Our midwife suggested that since we were on the mainland anyway, maybe we could go to her place up near Dover-Foxcroft and wait there; her husband was home and could help us as well. We climbed into the VW bus and headed for the woods inland. When we were almost there, I noticed suddenly that I was sitting in a puddle. My water had broken, and I began to feel the first dull ache of labor.

We pulled into our midwife's driveway to find that there was company. Her husband's old girlfriend's car was parked there, indicating that she had come to stay while our midwife was away. Needless to say, the scene did not look good. Since there was nobody home at present, we went in; Thomas and the midwife fixed a pallet on the floor for me.

Labor was slow and grinding. After all the books I had read, it wasn't until I was actively contracting that I realized that nothing had adequately described the *pain*. The books all seemed to extol the miracle of birth (O-how wonderful it was!) somehow, I had missed the part that said it was going to hurt like a son-of-a-bitch.

The afternoon dragged into evening and the labor pains just kept on coming. The midwife went to bed and Thomas waited up with me, breathing with me as each contraction turned my belly into a ball of fire. Around midnight the husband and his lady friend arrived. He was disturbed to find two strangers in his living room… one of whom was panting like a steam engine. When he found out his wife was back he looked very dismayed but tried to be cool about it. He retired to his bedroom to confront his wife, the lady friend and her little daughter went to the guest room, and the night stretched interminably on. I was able to doze on and off between contractions, but by morning things did not seem to have progressed much.

Everyone got up and had breakfast (but me) and the husband-midwife-girlfriend drama was skated around with great delicacy. I was unable to give it much attention because the contractions were coming harder and faster and the pain was starting to frighten me. At one point I looked up to see four adults and two small children clustered around, peering down at me. The adults were telling me to relax and stay calm. Easy for them to say when I was becoming increasingly certain that I was going to rip in two. I started to panic. The baby was ready to come but couldn't—he seemed to be stuck! I was unable to push, pull, or do anything except just *be* there—helplessly entangled in the tentacles of unspeakable pain. Finally, I broke down; I screamed and yelled and hollered and writhed on the floor. The midwife announced that it was time to go to the hospital NOW.

We piled into their little VW bug, with her husband driving, me in the front seat, and Thomas and the midwife in the back seat. He drove like a bat out of hell for the old Mayo hospital in Dover-Foxcroft. This was the one and only time in my life that I completely lost control of everything; that whole trip was one long horrible scream. The roads were bad, and we hit a lot of bumps and potholes. During one especially big thump I felt something change; something came loose inside me, and I realized, on the one still-functioning sub-level of my brain, that whatever was holding that baby back had just let go.

We screeched into the hospital parking lot and I was manhandled into the emergency room wailing like a banshee. I was plopped on the stretcher and a mask was slammed over my face. The doctor rushed in, quickly did an episiotomy and out slid a little boy, all in a rush. He was examined, weighed, and placed on my breast. The relief was beyond compare.

The doctor glared at Thomas who was standing crestfallen and meek in the room with us. While he stitched up my nether regions, this medical man proceeded to tell the father of my child exactly what he thought of him and his stupid ideas about home birthing with an underage girl in the middle of the Maine woods. I hardly noticed Thomas's humiliation because I was too busy examining the little pink

182

mouse-like creature on my chest blinking at me with deep blue eyes. I was just so fucking glad it was over.

The baby and I were wheeled into a room where forms were produced, and the hospital staff made ready for my incarceration. Thomas angrily strode into the room and said, "Can you walk?"

I replied, "Yes, I think so."

And so I did. We walked right out of the hospital not an hour after the baby was born with nurses chasing after us trying to get us to sign their forms. We went back to the midwife's house where Thomas brusquely thrust some money into her hands. We then mounted the VW bus with my tiny little bundle and headed back down the road.

We drove to Auburn. It was a long trip and it quickly became apparent that Thomas was furious with me. He was ready to go back and kill the doctor, that creep who sneered at him while sewing up my perineum. He raged about it nonstop, even suggested we just take the baby back and leave him. It had all gone wrong after all his careful planning, and the fault lay squarely on my shoulders. Why did I have to panic? Why did I let that doctor touch me? Why didn't I spit in his face or some other act of defiance? It was all totally fucked up and he would never forgive me nor let me forget it. I was crushed. I could do nothing but bend my head over the little sleeping body in my arms and watch my tears soak into the hospital-issued swaddling clothes.

By the time we got to his parents' house Thomas had lapsed into a sullen silence and scarcely acknowledged his parents' delight over their first grandchild. Thomas, the baby, and I stayed one night in the Chinese bed, where I had my first experience with a meconium bowel movement in the baby's diaper the following morning. We then headed back to the island, despite his parents begging us to stay a little longer to rest.

We had to spend another night at a motel before catching the morning boat and the baby screamed all night long. I was having trouble getting him to nurse—although I'd read all the books, nobody had showed me how it was done—and he just wailed and wailed while we walked him endlessly back and forth across the room. Thomas started to lose his cool during his turn and began shaking the tiny guy before I snatched him away, keeping him safe in my arms for the rest of the night.

Bleary-eyed we stumbled onto the island the next day amidst the bewildering congratulations of the islanders, all of whom wanted to see the tiny little being I was carrying in the sling on my front. I was astonished by the gifts that came pouring in; I knew nothing of baby presents or showers. We stayed at the Summer Cottage for a week while I recuperated and then headed back to our little island to take up our lives as new parents.

My newborn baby

We were having some difficulty deciding on a name for the baby. Thomas's choices were either Kazar or Conan, after barbarian comic book heroes. Those names were perfectly horrible in my opinion, so I put my foot down. I had always loved whales and since "Sperm" wasn't such a good choice, I picked from the Latin *Orcinus orca*—Orca the killer whale. This, I decided, would be a sufficiently strange and interesting name for our infant. After the word got out about the naming, a visitor told me that they'd heard the baby's name was "Aw-Kah", that being the true Maine pronunciation and indeed, how Orca's name would be pronounced on Monhegan from then on.

Orca was a colicky, fussy baby and when he wasn't crying, he was throwing up. When he wasn't doing those two things, he was pooping and peeing. We only had cloth diapers, so soon I was faced with a laundry monster of epic proportions. The baby had me up several times a night and could not seem to get happy. I quickly took over all his care when it became obvious to me that Thomas couldn't be trusted with him. Orca rode in his baby backpack as we made our treks across the harbor, apparently only happy when he was moving somewhere.

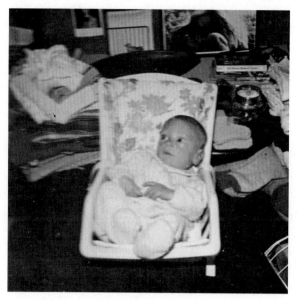

Orca

As the weeks went by I noticed that my baby seemed to be awfully thin and while he was getting longer, he wasn't getting any thicker. He also vomited up almost all the milk he nursed, often sending a white projectile stream seven or eight feet across the room. While thumbing through the Dr. Spock baby manual, I came across a description of pyloric stenosis and knew immediately that this was what was wrong. Orca's pyloric sphincter had swelled up to the extent that it had blocked the exit for his stomach and very little in the way of nourishment was getting through.

We took the next boat inshore and went to see a pediatrician. The doctor was extremely concerned about our baby. He explained that Orca had lost weight, was dehydrated and needed immediate surgery.

Our little six-week-old was admitted into the hospital that night and his operation was scheduled for the next day. I was unable to feed my baby before surgery, so the doctor suggested I go to my in-laws for the night. I left the hospital with my breasts leaking and aching, returning early the next morning to anxiously pace the waiting room during the interminable wait for him to get out of surgery. He was fine and, aside from a large incision under his rib cage held neatly together with internal stitches, he looked like nothing had happened. It took a while for his stomach to start accepting milk normally, but he nursed hungrily and soon began to gain weight again.

We arrived back on our little island and I immediately got a raging, horrendously painful case of mastitis in both of my breasts. They became hard, fiery-hot cannonballs that could only be relieved by nursing, the act of which was beyond excruciating. I struggled through it, nursing Orca with tears streaming down my face, determined to feed my baby the natural way.

We settled into a routine of trying to prepare ourselves for the upcoming winter. There was firewood to row across the harbor, little pens to build for the five goats we had bought, hay to be ordered from the mainland and hauled across the harbor, endless fixing and winterizing of our shacks. We got as much done as was possible with a small baby, and with mandatory breaks to get stoned. I soon found that very little got done when we were high and when Thomas pulled out his pot pipe, the day was as good as over.

Thomas frequently reminded me that he was still angry and disappointed in me about Orca's birth and therefore justified in his periodic dislike of our baby and his unwillingness to love him fully. He also voiced suspicions that Orca was probably not really his son after all; I had likely been screwing around in California and was probably thinking I was being clever in foisting this baby off on him. He simply ignored the fact that Orca was his spitting image.

I had finally figured out that there were good days and bad days. If Thomas was having a good day, then all was well. He was happy, loving, and fun. If it was a bad day, then all was shit. He would accuse me, berate me, and beg me to just tell him that: a) I was unfaithful to him, b) I desired other men all the time, c) Orca really wasn't his child, or d) I wasn't a virgin when he first seduced me.

"Come on," he'd beseech me, "Just tell me and then I'll know. I'll forgive you, but you just have to TELL me."

I knew that there were times I had to lie to protect myself, like about the boyfriend I had when I was fourteen who kissed me, but even *I* knew better than to tell lies that would incriminate me. So, I would sit miserably during these inquisitions, begging him to understand that all these fantasies were untrue, helplessly waiting for it to pass.

Up to this point, all of Thomas's attacks on me had been verbal, but during our first year on Manana, this changed. On one of his down days, his paranoia started to escalate beyond where I could placate him. Suddenly he swung out with his fist, hitting me hard on the side of the face. My head snapped back, and I fell from my chair onto the floor. He stood over me threateningly while I cowered and cried. Finally, he stormed out of the house, rowed across the harbor to Monhegan, and didn't return until later in the day. When he came back he attempted to erase the bad event and with an almost manic intensity that was impossible to resist. He would not apologize or promise it wouldn't happen again, he simply pretended nothing had happened at all, overbalancing on the side of being the most loving, caring, best man on earth. Later more blows would fall, and I would be hit, punched, and kicked, and each time he pretended afterwards that nothing had happened.

Like other battered women, I believed that my partner's behavior was my fault. If I hadn't argued, or if I hadn't said something wrong, I somehow could have averted it. I would always persevere, for the time when all would be good again, when peace would finally descend on our lives. There were calms before the storms, followed by a rage that, like a giant wave, would wash over my existence, drowning me in fear, pain, and shame.

Whenever I would look out the window of our Manana home, I would pray for peaceful seas. Flat-ass-calm is what we called it. It was a time when not a ripple disturbed the surface, and all was in a state of rest. These were the best conditions for crossing our harbor, when we would be least likely to get hurt.

But there was always a certain knowledge that under the placid surface of the waters, there were hidden powers that were just waiting to erupt and destroy this illusion of tranquility. Like our little island, perched in the middle of a maelstrom of weather and tides, so was my life; swirling like a dust mote caught in the upheavals of our marriage. I always craved the calm, and I just never knew when things would go to hell.

Manana Sojourner

CHAPTER TWENTY ~ UNFORGIVING ISLAND

Common sense is not so common.

—Voltaire

Early one autumn morning, when Orca was about 4 months old, I rowed Thomas across to Monhegan, so he could do a small job for someone. To support us he found odd jobs here and there, helping with carpentry work or small welding projects that kept us afloat financially. He instructed me to return to Manana and come back to pick him up late that afternoon.

As the day wore on, I noticed that the wind was picking up from the southwest and the harbor began to look less hospitable with each passing hour. By the appointed time in the afternoon, the winds were gale force and the seas in the harbor were about four to five feet high. Lobster boats were plunging on their moorings, and the waves rolled on through the harbor, only to crash onto the rocky face of Smutty Nose and up against the wharf.

This was to be my first rough crossing since we'd moved to Manana that summer. We didn't have a radio or any way I could contact Thomas to make other arrangements, and I knew better than to disobey his instructions, so I strapped the baby to my front and went down to the launch area where our skiff was tied. The tide was halfway out, and as I pushed the skiff down the rocks, I noticed with some trepidation that there were heavy rollers crashing into the spot where I was supposed to launch. I waited for the right moment because I knew I wasn't going to get a second chance to get this right. I didn't know at the time that I was being observed by a group of fishermen on the other side, who were congregated in a fish house and dumbfounded that I was even going to attempt this crossing.

Jay Hall Connaway (1893-1970) "Monhegan Rocks" (Elijah Bosley)

Those who live on the sea believe in the theory of the seventh wave. Waves follow a pattern: several smaller waves, followed by one significantly larger, more powerful wave. This is called the seventh wave, even though in reality, it may be the fifth wave or even the tenth. I waited for the seventh wave because a large wave would be most likely to carry me out beyond the point where the next wave would form; to take a smaller wave prior to a large wave was a recipe for disaster.

The big wave finally appeared, and as it hit the rocks and flowed up to its highest point, I pushed the skiff stern-first into it and jumped aboard, all in one smooth motion. I clambered to the center seat and had my oars in the locks in a matter of seconds, while I was being carried out by the ebb of the wave. I push-rowed as hard as I could and got past the next wave that was rushing in. I then turned the skiff and began the long row across the harbor. Orca bounced around on my chest throughout all this activity but didn't utter a peep.

I began navigating across the harbor, where the waves were definitely the biggest I'd ever rowed through. In those days the boat moorings were made up of a long heavy chain anchored to a huge rock on the bottom of the harbor at one end, and attached with a large iron staple to a ten-foot tree trunk at the other end that acted as a float to which boats were attached via a smaller tethering chain. These mooring stumps, as they were called, were painted with red copper paint and a white cap and would sink below the surface as each roller came over it, only to thrust up out of the water like a piston as the wave went past. They were to be avoided at all cost, as were the heaving lobster boats and their tethering chains, which were abruptly pulled out of the water with each tug of the waves. All this harbor clutter had to be wended through with care as I climbed each wave and went down into each trough in a frightening swoop, but my progress was steady, and I was a strong rower.

Fish Beach, whose breakwater afforded it a small measure of protection, was the only beach calm enough to land at. As I approached, I noticed a few people had come out to wait for my arrival. I neared the beach, but I needed to wait for the best wave to ride in on so as to not be caught short and risk having the next wave come in and swamp the skiff. I rode in and the skiff was grabbed by the men and hauled quickly above the reach of the next onslaught of water.

I climbed out of the boat and faced the fishermen, some of whom were white with anger at my stupidity in risking the lives of the two of us in this way. But they didn't say as much to me; they just helped me haul my skiff up the beach and watched me walk away. They reserved their censure for Thomas, and he got an earful about it later.

Winter arrived, and before we knew it we found ourselves isolated in our tiny shack on our tiny island with no one but ourselves for company. There was a Coast Guard station over the hill with two men on duty at all times, and we quickly made friends with the lonely, unhappy young men who would rather be anyplace in the world than on that godforsaken rock. These young men, assigned on rotating temporary duty, were from all over the country and most had very little knowledge of boats or tides. More than once we were asked for help in retrieving their canoe-shaped craft, known as a "peapod," from certain disaster when they tried to cross the harbor on ill-advised days.

George Bellows (1882-1925) "Beating out the Sea" 1913

The coasties took to visiting us regularly to share a joint or just break up the monotony of their time on the island. Once there were two men stationed together who absolutely hated each other's guts, so they would take turns visiting us to get away from each other. We would pay them a visit sometimes too—to watch TV or bask in the comfort of the fully electrified and warm station, the drone of huge generators always in the background. During a fog it was a pretty uncomfortable place, since the foghorn was situated right outside their door and blasted out a deafening honk every minute or so.

It was through our friendship with the coasties that we were able to get electricity for our house. The station generators were always running to power the foghorn, the Loran signal and, through a cable snaked across the harbor, Monhegan's lighthouse. It produced far more power than they could use, so it was just a matter of burying a long wire from their little winch house at the top of the hill down to our shacks and plugging in for us to enjoy the same luxury. It was great. We could have lights and even a little electric heater. Thomas immediately figured we could get some grow lights and have our own year-round marijuana crop. Quickly we walled off a little room to start that venture. But our bright lights shone like a beacon, alerting the residents of Monhegan that we were no longer seeing by the glow of kerosene. One of the islanders, an ex-coastie, ratted us out, and it wasn't long before a visiting CO yanked our cord—plunging us back into darkness.

Manana Fog Signal Station (USCG)

We started to run out of money. Whatever summer savings we had accumulated began to evaporate quickly, and since Thomas refused to stern on a lobster boat, we had no winter income. We had to live from dive to dive on lobster boats to stay solvent.

We took to sneaking up over the hill to the Coast Guard station in the dark of night to pilfer diesel fuel from their storage tanks to burn in our Aladdin space heaters. We'd venture out about once a week in the freezing stinging wind, feeling our faces start to go numb with frostbite as we struggled up the almost perpendicular hill through the snow drifts, hauling our five-gallon cans, hearts pounding with the fear of being caught. I'd nervously stand watch while Thomas filled the cans, slowly, slowly—it took so long! Then we would stagger under their weight, stinking diesel fuel sloshing on our hands and clothes as we struggled down over the icy hill to home. The Aladdin heaters were meant to burn kerosene and the diesel stank horribly with fumes that made our eyes water—likely coating our lungs with carcinogenic crud—but it was free, so we lived with it.

The only way we really survived at all was with well-timed gifts of money from parents and in-laws that allowed us to buy some groceries and get by. Our plan was to start making cheese from the goat's milk that would soon be flowing from our now-pregnant nannies. This we would sell at the store across the way, and we were sure it would sustain us nicely.

We would buy many books every time we visited the mainland. These were mostly books on alternative animal husbandry, alternative home building, alternative healthcare, alternative farming practices and other encouragements to our alternative lifestyle. We read science fiction, because Thomas loved it. I didn't really care—if there was a book in the vicinity I would read it—reading was my sole form of entertainment.

Once, during one of her many moves, my mother sent me all her books from California. There were boxes of them, all of which we lugged down to the Summer Cottage. Thomas sorted through the books, decided which ones were proper reading for us, and burned the rest. Any books that mentioned sex or were abridged in anyway were relegated to the fire. It was with no little sadness that I watched *An ABZ of Love* curl up into ash. He also got in the habit of burning any toys of Orca's that did not fall into his guidelines of what constituted proper playthings. Plastic was considered unsuitable for Orca's development, so our stove received a lot of brightly colored beads, rings, and assorted other baby things that had the bad taste to be constructed of plastic.

No matter how poor we were, we always seemed to have plenty of marijuana on hand. Getting stoned every day was a ritual for us and anyone who visited was instantly offered a pipe. One day an unusually large supply of frozen bananas from the store arrived so I decided to

194

make some pot banana bread. I mixed all the ingredients together, shaking a largish amount of marijuana into the mix. I figured this would last us for days since each slice would be enough for a pretty good buzz. The bread came out of the oven redolent of weed and bananas—a mixture that still makes me ill even to think of—and soon we partook of our first slice.

Unfortunately, the munchies hit with a vengeance soon after and with the single-minded idiocy that accompanies this urge, Thomas and I quickly consumed the entire loaf. What followed was a long, dreary episode of marijuana poisoning the likes of which I'd never experienced before nor since. Soon we were both prostrate on the floor as if we were nailed there, unable to do anything but watch the room spin endlessly around in a thoroughly sickening fashion. It took hours to wear off and while this experience didn't stop us from smoking grass, I never baked with it again.

We'd often get visitors to our little place on Manana. People "visited" a lot in those days, always arriving unannounced because there were no telephones; it wasn't surprising to look out and see a skiff wending its way across the harbor toward Manana on a calm day. We'd always break out the pipe, and whatever food I might have on hand to offer to our guests. One day we were visited by a couple of young sternmen and we cranked up the stove to warm the house. After a while I excused myself to head to the outhouse; I'd also been partaking of the pipe and was pretty stoned as well. As I walked through the barn on the way to the privy, I heard a crackling sound. I looked up to see that where the stovepipe emerged from the building, small flames ate at the siding of the house. Thomas had neglected to place any sheet metal around the pipe to keep its hot sides from touching dry wood and our house was in the beginning stages of burning down. I calmly walked back into our living room and said in an almost deadpan voice, "The house is on fire and you'd better do something about it."

Everyone looked at me with disbelief, but finally the message filtered through and they all sprang into action; buckets were fetched, and the fire was put out before it spread.

The view out our window was of the harbor, with Monhegan as a backdrop. I spent much of my time gazing at this scene, watching the lobstermen put their boats on and off the moorings and noting the tides.

Tides were an integral part of life on an island. The deeper into the Gulf of Maine you go, the more extreme the tides, with those in the Bay of Fundy in New Brunswick, Canada, being the most tremendous.

Shacks on Manana (Abby Sewall)

Monhegan's tides were around nine feet from low to high and the phenomenon of the changing of tides always put a very different light on the place. High tides were easier for crossing the harbor since only seaweed-free rocks presented themselves and we didn't have to drag our skiff as far up the beach on the other side. Low tide exposed the underbelly of the harbor, the rockweed lay lank and flat on the rocks, and the beaches became larger expanses of sand and pebbles. Low tide was a time for picking mussels; I eagerly hunted for the blue mollusks hiding beneath the seaweed, wrestling them from their tight grip on the rocks that anchored them securely against the turbulence of the waters.

There was always a little danger involved with eating mussels during the summer months because of the possibility of red tide. Red tide is billions of small critters called dinoflagellates that proliferate during certain favorable conditions, congregating in the gut of clams and mussels to release a neurotoxin that can paralyze your respiratory muscles. The local wives' tale was that if you felt your lips tingling while eating mussels you should stop immediately, thus avoiding the gruesome prospect of going into respiratory failure. I was never able to test this theory, though I did eat lots of mussels.

Tides follow a pattern that can be predicted with great accuracy. Tide calendars, published each year, were an important reference for us. Not only did they tell the exact time of high and low tide (generally the tides advanced about an hour each day so high tide at noon on Monday would be followed by high tide around one o'clock on Tuesday), but the actual height of the tide itself was also forecast. Tides were dictated by the pull of the sun and moon. During full and new moons there would usually be bigger tides, known as spring tides. Between the phases of the moon were the weaker neap tides. At certain times of year when the sun and moon were in alignment there would be even higher and lower tides than usual, often rising and falling several feet above and below the normal heights.

It was during a heavy spring tide in February of 1978 that one big storm hit. I had noticed the day before that the tides were unusual. More of the harbor bottom was exposed; places where I would have had to wade to collect mussels were now high and dry. The pink calcification that coated the rocks on the bottom of the harbor was visible above the water line. At high tide the water crept up almost to the grass line on Manana. Weather radios were as much a part of life as tide calendars and the forecast that night was for a heavy gale from the southeast. That gale turned into what is now known as the Blizzard of '78.

That night our little shacks shook horribly as the screaming wind flew by. This was more than just a gale; it was a storm with hurricane-force winds. The coasties later told us that their anemometer had reached over ninety-eight miles an hour. It was dark and wild, with snow flying by horizontally, not even bothering to touch down. We hunkered in our fragile hovel praying that we wouldn't end up in pile of rubble by morning.

Finally, the early morning light filtered in and I looked out. Something was different about Monhegan; there were fewer fish houses on the beach and the ones that remained had large gaping holes in them. One entire building had disappeared; its contents of rope and gear were strewn across the rocks of the entire western shore of the island. There were miles of bright yellow polypropylene trap warp snaking like cables from one end of the harbor to the next. The Coast Guard boathouse on our side was half gone. The wharf on Monhegan was a merely a shell of granite blocks with the slip thrown up and off to the side and the pilings strewn around like pickup-sticks. The harbor was still boiling with masses of high rollers crashing onto and over Smutty Nose; it was several days before the mail boat could run again. No boats were lost, which was a small miracle, but it was a long time and many disaster relief dollars later before all was put right again.

Winslow Homer (1836-1919) "Northeaster". Ca. 1895

During the winter the rockweed would freeze at low tide, becoming stiff and brittle, and a thick sheet of ice would mark the high tide mark. It was hazardous business getting the skiff down the rocks because the rockweed, slippery by nature at any time, was even slicker when coated with ice.

On a particularly cold and miserable day when the mercury was down in the minus numbers, Thomas decided to do a dive he'd been asked to perform a few days before. I thought he was crazy; it was way too cold, and you could hardly see Monhegan from the vapor issuing forth from the harbor's surface like a giant steaming cauldron. The lobster boats were all coated with a thick layer of ice that started at the waterline and covered the entire hull, dripping like runny vanilla icing off the mooring chains.

Once Thomas got an idea in his mind, there was very little I, or anyone else could do to sway him. Soon he was struggling into his wetsuit, checking his tanks and gear, and rowing himself out across the harbor to the boat he was supposed to dive on. It was one of those days when you feel your face is going to freeze off the minute you step outside and it was with no little anxiety that I watched him go.

As soon as he launched himself backward off his skiff into the water, he knew he'd made a big mistake. The plastic frame holding his air tank had not been designed for this kind of temperature extremes, so it immediately cracked in two when he hit the water, allowing his tank to float loose. His regulator froze solid, making it impossible for him to breathe. The water temperature was only about twenty-eight degrees and its paralyzing numbness rapidly seeped into the zipper openings and gaps in the wetsuit.

Somehow, he struggled back into the skiff and started rowing as fast as he could back to Manana. His wet neoprene diving gloves immediately coated with ice, and he could not maintain a grip on the oars. Soon his entire wetsuit was freezing into a shell of ice; with great fear, he could feel the beginnings of hypothermia stealthily creeping into his body. It was a case of row or die. Frantically he pulled the gloves off with his teeth and started for home, rowing barehanded.

It was his screams that alerted me that something was wrong. I threw on a coat, dashed down the hill, slipping on ice and snow, nearly falling into the harbor myself as he hove into view. He was crying and yelling, his hands now frozen to the oars. When he finally made it close enough for me to grab the painter on the bow of the skiff, I hauled him in. I helped him remove his claw-like hands from the oars and supported him up the hill to warmth and safety.

Thomas was lucky. He had a horrific case of frostbite on both of his hands and they soon blistered and peeled in the same way they would have if they had been burned. He was forever after particularly sensitive to cold in those extremities, but he was alive. Even he had to admit that this was one of the stupidest things he had ever done.

FLAT ASS CALM

CHAPTER TWENTY-ONE ~
HOMESTEADING FOR DUMMIES

*Whatever women do, they must do twice as well as men
to be thought half as good.
Luckily, this is not difficult.*

—*Charlotte Whitton*

Spring finally arrived, and we were beset with damp, chilly weather. The islands were on a major bird flyway and each spring and fall saw thousands of brightly colored, twittering feathered friends passing through. They were quickly followed by hundreds of birdwatchers who stalked Monhegan in groups, binoculars firmly planted against their eyeballs, pausing only to emit strange bird-like sounds in the hopes of enticing a rare warbler to show itself. All the island cats looked forward to this time of year with great anticipation; the exhausted little birds made easy prey, and the local felines slaughtered the avian tourists in large numbers.

A stray blade or two of grass began to poke through and the sun was just starting to have some warmth to it, but springtime on the Maine islands was generally a long, slow, drawn-out affair. We'd wait endlessly for that time when summer would swoop in suddenly in late June, only to discover she was only going to hang around just long enough to make us think we could be warm again, before rushing out of our lives to make way for fall.

Orca was growing into a large healthy toddler who walked at eight months. He was a very handsome blond child who looked just like his father. I soon found to my disgust that his favorite snack was goat turds. I would set him down outside for a minute and come back to find him with a mouthful of brown berries that were quickly turning into a goo of shit, dribbling down his chin. I would frantically try to scoop it out, cursing myself for being such a bad mother, praying fervently that he wouldn't die from this dreadfulness. As horrible as it was, he didn't seem to suffer any bad effects from it.

Orca

When spring finally came, I accomplished his toilet training by simply sending him outside like a little dog to pee and poop. His housebreaking went very well, except for the time or two that he only got as far as the front step before depositing his little pile of shit. Woe unto anyone who didn't step carefully coming into our house.

The goat's bellies became large and their udders pendulous with the upcoming kidding looming into sight. We read books on how to care for them during labor and delivery and felt quite prepared for the event. The goats were docile animals whose warm grassy breath was sweet and comforting. We'd borrowed a buck goat in the fall to breed our does and once he had performed his job, he was returned to his owner on the mainland.

Watching goats breed is a singular experience that is not for the weak at heart. The billy, with his hair sticking up all over—stinking like a rank skunk—would prance stiff legged over to the does, his foot-long erection coyly tickling his chest. He would ritually urinate on his own beard to make himself smell nice for the ladies. That act seemed to be a major aphrodisiac because the does would immediately back up to him with their tails wagging like mad. The buck would then sample the lady's urine to ensure her readiness. After many bizarre grimaces and lip curls, he would mount his sweetheart and quickly consummate the act. Watching goats mate always left me quite certain that Satan was modeled after a goat for a very good reason.

The does had a definite pecking order and their lives were dictated by who was on top, not unlike my own life at the time. Their horns were their weapons and they didn't hesitate to use them. The goats didn't require too much winter care; we just threw hay a couple of times a day and chopped holes in the ice covering the little island pool for drinking water.

The first doe to go into labor was an older animal, and she seemed to be taking a rather long time about it. We waited and waited while she contracted and blatted. It finally became clear from her distress that something wasn't right. Since I had the smallest hands, I was elected to explore her internally to try to figure out what the problem was. I stuck my hand up her vagina, feeling for the opening of the cervix. Then I was able to insinuate my hand into her womb where I found a confusing assortment of slimy little hoofs and heads. It was like no other experience I'd ever had. I remember desperately thinking that in the book I'd read, *Raising Goats the Modern Way,* there was no mention of this kind of contingency; just some advice to go to a vet if things went wrong. I belatedly realized this constituted "things going wrong" and somehow, we'd forgotten that a vet wasn't to be had when we needed one.

The doe's contraction would come, she would cry out and her womb would tighten up like a vise leaving me unable to do a thing until it passed. Slowly I felt along and tried to organize in my mind what I was feeling in there; ok here was a leg and it was a front leg because the little hoof was pointed this way like so... then I would follow it along to the elbow and feel for the neck and the head, identifiable because of the eye sockets and the mouth, position it gently facing the cervix, then I'd feel down the other side of the head for the other leg... AHA! That one was pointed backward, so I had to reach back, now up to my shoulder in warm, wet, writhing goat, and find the little hoof, cup my hand over it and pull it forward, until it too was facing out——two little hoofs with a nose in between them... now a little tug during the next contraction and Whoop! Out came a baby goat, wet, slimy and alive. To my amazement I had to repeat this performance two more times on the same goat because she was carrying triplets, all turned the wrong way. It was a marvelous and exhilarating experience. With complete awe I watched the three little kids get up on weak wobbly legs and nuzzle their mother for a teat. Basking in Thomas's well-deserved admiration, I felt like a complete hero.

The other goats were able to manage without my assistance and soon we had a pen full of little kids and lactating mothers to contend with. We quickly separated the babies from their dams and started bottle-feeding them, so we could control the milking better.

This was when I learned how to milk a goat. If you want to have the world's best-developed forearms, I suggest you take up goat milking. Squeeze, squeeze, squeeze is all it is—that and contending with a sometimes-cantankerous animal who wants to kick over the bucket or put her foot in it.

The ladies would line up dutifully mornings and evenings, letting us know when we were late by their incessant baaing. According to strict pecking order, they would come into the milking room by twos, jump up on the milking benches and start eagerly eating the grain we placed in their bowls while we milked away. It was a satisfying job, milking. With my face pressed up against the warm sweet-smelling goat flank—the rhythmic thrum, thrum of milk hitting the side of the bowl—

I could dream gentle thoughts of placid waters and even convince myself that I enjoyed my life.

Me, with a bunch of kids

Generally, each doe would produce about a gallon of sweet, foamy, naturally homogenized milk a day. We would take the milk up to the kitchen, strain it and heat it on the stove until it reached the right temperature for cheese making. Then we'd add rennet (an enzyme from the stomach of a calf that curdles milk) and let it sit until a solid curd formed. When we determined that it was set we'd drain off the whey, add salt, and press the curds into homemade presses—leaving it to age a few days on a rack. We did this all without any refrigeration. If I wanted to keep milk cold I had to take it down to the harbor, pull in a little crate that was attached to a mooring off Manana's shore and keep it in there in bottles, bobbing gently in the harbor all day.

Thomas designed labels and called our business Barbarian Cheese Works. He had a great admiration of barbarians at the time, though I can't for the life of me remember why. Every day we'd row our product across the harbor where it sold very well in the store. As far as I know, nobody ever got sick; it really wasn't bad and lots of people complimented us on it. We were just thankful the health inspector never caught on.

I have no idea if we made enough money on this venture to survive or not. I was ignorant of even the smallest detail of our financial situation. Thomas had complete control of all money matters including keeping the checkbook balanced. Somehow, he knew when he had to go out and find more work to keep things going, and when he could let things slide. He would take odd jobs during each summer like carpentry or garbage collecting for the extra cash we needed to make ends meet. My responsibility was to take care of Orca, keep the house somewhat clean, and do my share of all the rest of the work involved.

We spent most of our money on animals. We soon had a good-sized herd of goats and a couple of sheep to start off a flock. We decided a donkey would be a good addition to our lives because he could haul rocks for us. We were very interested in the building techniques that involved using forms to contain a rock and cement mixture, as proposed by Helen and Scott Nearing over in Brooksville, Maine. Their book, *Living the Good Life,* was a bible for us and we admired them immensely. Thomas wanted us to build a house of our own on Manana. He had visions of underground structures made of stone and cement with little windows peeking out of the sod growing on the roof. In typical fashion, he chose the most inaccessible spot on the island for our building site; one that entailed trudging up two large cliffs to access it. Somehow, he managed to overlook the nearly impossible logistics of this big project. Like many of Thomas's plans, our stone house was one that never seemed to get off the ground.

We brought the donkey to Monhegan one day on the mail boat with lots of fanfare. We did have a bit of a puzzle trying to figure out how to transport him over to Manana, where there was no dock or landing of any kind suitable for this kind of animal. We loaded the patient beast onto a raft at high tide and he simply walked off onto the rocks at the other end.

That's how Jacques Derriere came to his new home. He was a sweet creature who had a lot of problems with his hoofs and, while we never found a use for him other than moving a few baskets full of rocks, I did learn a lot about how to care for his feet. Jacques also liked to bray, loudly. This noise would echo across the harbor and caused some annoyance on the part of the inn owner on Monhegan, who complained that the donkey was bothering his guests.

Jacques Derriere

We decided to try beekeeping too. One day the Monhegan postmaster sent word to us to get to her office immediately. There was a package there—angrily buzzing with its contents of an entire hive. We had mail-ordered bees and they had arrived. We'd bought used hives and decided to set them up on Monhegan where there was more shelter from the incessant winds. I soon became comfortable handling bees since they didn't seem to want to sting me, like they did Thomas. I would calmly open up the hives and pull out the combs, watching them crawl over my hands and up my arms. It was as though I had a kind of power over these tiny dangerous creatures. Strangely it left me feeling excited, yet humbled by my ability to touch them. The bees only lasted one season, sadly; the hives died off over the next winter.

Summer was a time of sweetness on Manana. The air was warm and gentle, the grass grew high, and the ocean sparkled with blinding specks of light that offset its incredible blueness. Orca, goat boy, was like a little waif of the island, running around joyously in totally naked splendor. I would take him out with me in the skiff and we would row around Manana, dragging a mackerel jig behind us. Tired and happy we would bring our fish home and roast them over an open fire.

Mackerel are fish that school together. You can find them by searching the water for their characteristic disturbance: a spot where it looks like wind is fluffing the surface where no wind should be. Often a gull would fly down and skim over a school, apparently just for the fun of seeing the fish boil the water in alarm at its appearance. Each fish is about a foot long, shaped like a thin, white-bellied torpedo, decorated with a beautiful pattern of black and iridescent blue markings on its back. I was always searching for mackerel schools, never hesitating to launch our skiff, weather and tide permitting, if I saw one off the backside of Manana. They were fun to catch, striking the lure with intensity, fighting bravely until hauled out of the water to their death. Their meat was dark, oily, and delicious when absolutely fresh.

Soon the leaves turned yellow on Monhegan's apple trees, the barberry bushes on the hills glowed red, and the fair-weather friends began to leave. The winds started blowing, making harbor crossings rougher, more dangerous. The official start of winter was when the mail boat started running only three days a week. Time to hunker down again in our little shack.

That fall a friend on Monhegan had brought home a young pig on an impulse—which he immediately regretted—so I ended up with a small female piglet named Blossom. She moved into the barn with the goats, chickens, sheep, rabbits, and donkey. Soon she was growing like a pig. We figured she'd be lonely and we brought home a young male pig we named Boardom to keep her company. I was amazed to find out that a pig's penis is shaped exactly like a very long, pink corkscrew. It was then that I finally knew with certainty where the term screwing came from. Soon we had a pregnant sow as well as numerous pregnant goats and sheep. The upcoming summer looked to be busy indeed.

Orca and Blossom

Thomas's bad days started to target Orca as well as me. Orca was never an easy child—full of beans, as they would say. He got into things, his first utterances were swear words, he threw tantrums and said no to everything first before he even knew what it was. He was a perfect target for Thomas's frustrations when I wouldn't do. I would try to stop it, desperately finding in me some way to overcome my own fear of being hurt while trying to protect my little boy.

I was unable to talk to anyone about how my life was; from the time I was very small I learned that I needed to keep secrets: the secret of my parent's divorce, my mother's drinking, my drug and alcohol use, and now my abusive marriage. These secrets were a necessary part of my survival, as important to me as life itself. Don't ask, don't tell, don't give yourself away. Thomas was safe because I would never tell on him, while Orca and I were never safe. Those who are abused often protect those who treat us the worst, maybe because this is all we know how to do.

On Monhegan there was a long-standing winter tradition of island women getting together once a week to knit and socialize. These get-togethers were called "knitting group" by the women, and "stitch and bitch" by their husbands. They provided me with a chance to get off my rock and spend some time with the island ladies. We discussed the weather or island gossip and whoever wasn't present was fair game. As one lady told me, "Nothing sweetens a nice cup of tea like sugar and scandal."

I already knew how to crochet and was soon learning the art of knitting as well. Each week a different hostess entertained us. She would prepare tea and try to outdo her predecessor in the baking department. I was predictably shy in this group; I could never have them over to my house to reciprocate. These get-togethers provided me with a chance to hear what was going on and bask in the company of women. Of course, I could never tell them what was *really* going on with me, but I still craved their company and I always prayed fervently for calm weather on stitch and bitch day.

CHAPTER TWENTY-TWO ~ GOAT HEADS AND ATTACK HELICOPTERS

The secret source of humor itself is not joy, but sorrow.
There is no humor in heaven.

—*Mark Twain*

Winters slid into springs and springs into summers. We had established our presence on our rock and became fixtures. We were a great topic of conversation for the tourists and islanders alike and could never forget our celebrity status. Trips inshore on the mail boat meant having to endure overhearing stories about ourselves being excitedly told by and to complete strangers. Many of the stories were untrue and, even by our standards, fantastical. Since our home was in complete view of the entire village of Monhegan, it was as if we were living on a stage to be watched, criticized, and commented on.

Thomas did his best to promote our mystique by doing as many outrageous things as he could to keep everyone talking. It almost appeared to be the sole reason for his existence, and he dearly loved being the center of attention. He slaughtered animals in full view of everyone, stalked around with a large knife strapped to his side, dressed in nothing but ragged shorts, and was sure to make frequent trips across the harbor to bask in the awed curiosity that radiated like a caressing beam of light from the other side.

Thomas had a fascination with goat skulls. He decorated our fence posts with the slaughtered goat's heads, giving our compound a strange primitive atmosphere. I'm sure the tourists wouldn't have been surprised if we emerged from our shacks dressed in goat skins and danced around a large bonfire at night. One particularly large head was obtained from a male goat that had been foisted off on us earlier that summer. This goat's testicles had never descended so he was effectively a neuter and we really had no use for him. We killed and butchered him, and Thomas set about figuring out how to preserve his impressive head with large horns swept back in a particularly graceful way. Instead of having to put up with the flies and stink of just letting it rot in the sun, Thomas thought up the ingenious idea of tying a rope around the horns and sinking the head to the bottom of the harbor to be picked clean by the crabs and other invertebrates that lived there.

Manana Goat

My brother, Frank, owned the nearest mooring to our shore and we would often tie a crate to it in which to store milk, mussels, crabs, or lobsters. Frank had a little sailboat moored there as well. Thomas rowed out one day and sank the tethered goat's head off the mooring, tying it carefully to our little crate.

About a week later I was sitting outside in the sunshine watching Frank as he rowed across the harbor to his boat. He was going out for a sail and he climbed on board to make everything ready before casting off. As he was getting ready to put his skiff on the mooring, he spied the rope tied to our lobster crate, trailing off toward the bottom of the harbor. Curiosity got the better of him and I watched with bated breath as he slowly pulled the rope up hand over hand. When what must have been a particularly gruesome sight finally came into full view, complete with its little ascending bubbles of putrefaction gasses, I waited to see how he would react. He simply released his hold on the rope and stared dumbstruck as the partially decomposed goat head fell back to the bottom. Then he went about his business of going out for a sail and never mentioned the incident to us. I used to think my brother was a little strange.

My brother Will, who was also a little odd, would often visit us when he was summering on the island. He worked at Harvard University, where he was immersed in the B.F. Skinner approach to psychology. Will was a thin, bearded guy with a dry wit. His work consisted of running rats and pigeons through Skinner boxes, with computerized programs testing various forms of positive and negative reinforcement. Once he brought us a bunch of white pigeons whose brains were totally fried from all the pecking at bright lights they had to do endlessly for their food. They fluttered around Manana and Monhegan for a while, invoking many comments from the bewildered islanders before they finally all died. We drew the line at Will bringing any more animals after he showed up with a few addled rats.

I was rowing Will across the harbor to Manana one day when one of the more loud and obnoxious fishermen threw a codfish into our skiff, "for our supper." Thomas had expressly forbidden me from ever accepting gifts from most of the lobstermen in general; his pride dictated that we not become beggars of seafood while on our many trips across the harbor. This fisherman was one Thomas particularly disliked but, being the polite person I was, I didn't know how to possibly refuse the gift. It was with some panic I told Will of my predicament and he agreed to say that he had procured the fish himself to bring as a gift. We brought home the fish and I cleaned it, inviting Will to stay for dinner. As we sat down to eat, Thomas asked Will how he had gotten the fish. There was a long pause and I realized with horror that Will had failed to formulate a convincing fish alibi.

"I, uh, found it on the beach," he blurted out.

I groaned internally, but Will had warmed up to his improbable story. "Well, yes, you see I was just walking along the beach and there was this fish! It looked OK to me, so I said to myself, why not have it for dinner?"

Thomas surveyed the food on his plate that he had just been told was garbage found on the beach. Good manners won out, however, and he replied faintly, "far out."

One summer Thomas got a job working on the garbage scow. This was a lobster boat that waited at the end of the wharf at an appointed time at the end of the day and received all of the island's trash to be hauled out a couple of miles and thrown overboard. This job presented a perfect opportunity to start collecting stuff. Thomas believed he was an artist at heart, and while he had done some good small welded sculptures in the past, he hadn't produced any artwork in a very long time. Now he had a way to obtain all sorts of interesting raw materials for future projects; future projects that were never started, much less completed. Our yard soon filled up with bits and pieces of scrap metal, old furniture, and a strange assortment of junk. While Thomas and the tourists on Monhegan may have thought at the time that this was all very colorful and cute, I was becoming uncomfortably aware that we were living like hicks, complete with appliances in the yard and our grubby little boy squatting bare-bottomed in the dirt.

My dog Alice also contributed to Monhegan's entertainment by being a true wonder dog in her own right. Alice was a mutt who would not tolerate being left behind. She had an extreme form of separation anxiety and there was no way she could be left in a house or car without tearing apart whatever she was imprisoned in. Our VW bus soon had streamers of fabric and upholstery hanging throughout it from her frantic attempts to get out and she would chew through any collar, rope, or harness if we tried to tie her up to leave her home. Alice probably broke all records for any dog swimming across the harbor between Monhegan and Manana—winter or summer—and no matter how sneaky we tried to be, we could never fool her into staying home. Since we often tied our skiff at the wharf when visiting Monhegan, she soon learned that if she didn't want to be left in the skiff, she had to learn to climb the ladder that went straight up the side. Up she would go, propelling her front legs up to the next rung and following behind with her back legs. She rarely toppled over and within a year or so she was a real pro at it. She never could learn how to go down, so we had to carry her or pick her up off the rocks, where she patiently waited for us.

On the wharf with Orca and Alice

Alice's main pleasures in life were barking at men and fetching things, but mostly fetching things. She would hound you endlessly with a stick or a ball to be thrown and once it was tossed, she immediately brought it back for another throw, over and over and over again. There was no end to her enjoyment of this game. I took to throwing her sticks in hard-to-fetch places, like up in trees, but she would just climb the tree to get it and bring it back. Often people on Monhegan would be dumbstruck to see Alice way up in a tree jumping from branch to branch to fetch her stick. When we were on the cliffs on the backside of Monhegan I would amuse myself by throwing the stick off Whitehead or Blackhead. Then I would time Alice in her mad scramble to the bottom and back up to the top of these nearly vertical behemoth rock headlands, with the stick always clutched firmly in her jaws. Yes, Alice truly was the wonder dog of the islands.

Orca on Manana on a foggy day (John Schick)

The Coast Guard station over the hill was in its beginning stages of becoming automated. Soon there would be no more coasties to keep us company during the winter, a prospect that we didn't entirely feel badly about. Some of the guys had become tiresome and their constant visits were beginning to be viewed with the same enthusiasm we would have shown a Jehovah's Witness knocking at our door. There were big doings underway to bring out all the needed equipment to do this changeover in what turned out to be a years-long process

One day I was walking up the hill from our house enjoying the soft summer day. Orca was perched on my hip and we were saying hi to a couple of goats when suddenly a huge helicopter rose into view in front of us. It was one of the really big ones, with two gigantic overhead rotors, and it was being used to haul especially heavy equipment to the island. Like all the other curious tourists, the pilot decided to come take a look at our home. Before I knew it, the goats had vanished, and Orca and I were slammed to the ground by the intense force of the propeller wash under the massive machine. There were rocks, stones, and dirt flying around us. Orca was screaming with fear and I likely was too. After it passed us by, I watched that awesome machine advance over our shacks, while shingles, boards and rocks flew around in gay abandon and the chickens rolled down the hill like bowling balls. It was like an explosion in a shingle factory. Finally, they moved off and after I picked the dirt, stones, and grass out of my mouth, I stormed up over the hill to confront the bastards. I was steamed. The poor guy who was in charge at the station didn't know what to think of the disheveled, dirty, wild-haired young woman, complete with crying child, who was waving her arms and babbling about being attacked by helicopters. I think I got my point across though, and they left us alone after that.

FLAT ASS CALM

CHAPTER TWENTY-THREE ~ THE RESTLESS JERK

No adultery is bloodless.

—*Natalia Ginzburg*

It was spring again. Our sow had a large litter of piglets so another one of our chores included hauling the Island Inn's daily kitchen slops across the harbor to feed them. Someone found an orphaned fawn and gave it to us; he survived for a while on goat's milk, and then mysteriously died, I suspect from neglect. We milked about twenty goats a day and produced many pounds of cheese that needed to be wrapped and sold. We rarely had time to do anything else. The smell of ripening goat cheese started to make my stomach heave, and I knew I was pregnant again.

We were both glad another child was on the way. We wanted Orca to have a sibling and it was with the same complete certainty, as before, that I knew that this one would be a girl. I'd weaned Orca and he was completely housebroken—er, potty trained—by this time, so the prospect of a second child did not seem overwhelming. I felt myself growing bigger, clumsier and started having terrible back pains from the pregnancy. Suddenly I would have a knifing twinge down my back; literally causing me to collapse. Thomas accused me of being a baby and faking my episodes, but they were real. I knew then that pregnancy was not my thing. I secretly started making plans to avert any future occurrences of this condition.

My old high school friend Sarah came out that summer to work at the store. She was going to stay with my brother Frank at his house. Unfortunately, she immediately got into a fight with him and he threw her out. Having no place else to go, she came over to Manana to live with us. Thomas would row her to work across the harbor every day. These rides soon disintegrated into Thomas shamelessly coming on to Sarah the whole way, trying to convince her to sleep with him. It embarrassed the hell out of her and one day she finally told me about it. I could only mumble that I was sorry and begged her to just ignore his advances. I was horrified by his behavior. When I finally got up the courage to confront Thomas about it later, he brushed me off, explaining with complete seriousness that Sarah *really* wanted to have sex with him. Her telling me about it was merely a way of asking for permission. He was a bit annoyed that I hadn't been amenable to his adultery.

Thomas's newest and most pervasive fantasy was of himself lording over two women. He didn't try to hide this from me; instead he endlessly tried to convince me to come over to his way of thinking. He would have preferred if both his partners were bisexual, performing their lovemaking in front of him as well as with him. I was not interested in the slightest. Since I have never had the slightest attraction to female genitalia—not to mention being horribly jealous—I was a lousy candidate for this scenario. This caused Thomas no end of disappointment, but since all the cards were now on the table, he felt no qualms about actively taunting me by pursuing other women; I would just have to put up with it. The idea that I would reciprocate and take a lover myself was unthinkable. Like the King of Siam, Thomas was the honeybee who was allowed to sample all the flowers, while I had to keep myself for him alone.

One day he went over to Monhegan and I was surprised when he didn't come home that night. When I learned later that he had spent the night on Monhegan with his old girlfriend Crystal, I was crushed. I had operated to this point under the illusion that our mutual fidelity was a rock that I could cling to when all else failed. Now that it was gone I had very little left. I felt lower than a worm.

So, we got married.

Coupled with all the other insanity, Thomas, on one of his descending moods, suddenly decided that he was tired of Manana and we were going to immigrate to Canada. His oldest sister had married a Canadian and they lived in St. Andrews, New Brunswick. Thomas's newest scheme involved buying our own island there, with what money I knew not. There we would live true lives of isolation and freedom. In his new, feverish desire to relocate, magically leaving all our troubles behind, he happily ignored the fact that the only things that kept him going were the endless streams of attention from Monhegan's adoring tourists, the sanctuary of Tim and Marie's home, and the trips to his parents' house on the mainland.

Rockwell Kent (1882-1971) "Down to the Sea" 1910

We couldn't apply for Canadian residency without being married, so one day we found ourselves standing nervously in the old postmaster's living room with a couple of friends. We were quite a sight, both barefoot, with our little boy looking on, and me obviously pregnant, while Winnie of "et yer pickle yet?" fame stumbled over the stilted marriage ceremony.

Of course, nothing else would change, there were no rings, and I kept my name. Although our new child would be able to have Thomas's name, we were essentially exactly as we were before. Neither of us really believed in marriage; I was sure that all of them were doomed to failure, but we told ourselves that this was just a necessary step toward our moving to Canada, so it would all be okay.

Married life went on exactly like unmarried life… only things got worse. Thomas started actively courting other women on Monhegan, leaving me home alone with a growing belly and an aching heart. I felt completely powerless to do anything about it. Thomas had pointed out to me over and over again that his straying was my fault because I was frigid. This, he explained, diminished him as a man, leaving him with no other option but to find his pleasure elsewhere. I was expected to be a good sport about it and would sit gritting my teeth as he happily told me about his latest prospects. Fortunately, he had few, if any, conquests after his brief encounter with Crystal, for which I was very grateful. Summer was slipping away and soon there would be winter with no new young birds around for him to prey on.

As fall came and the weather started to get worse, there was one young woman who stayed on Monhegan longer than most. Maybe she was interested in Thomas too, or was just staying on the island for her own reasons but she gave me real reason to worry. The day before she was due to leave, it was rough in the harbor, but Thomas knew that this would be his last chance to convince her to stay longer. He was determined to row across to her and I had to go help him launch the skiff off our rock.

The seas were high, likely four footers, and they whooshed into our little landing area with foamy intensity. As with all our rough water launches off the island, we knew we had to time this one perfectly because there was very little room for error. We both pushed the skiff with all our might and Thomas jumped in to ride the wave out, but one of the chafing strips on the bottom of the boat had come loose and was hanging down like a grappling hook. The skiff stopped short, hung up precariously on a rock, leaving Thomas high and dry and directly in the path of the next roller coming in. The wave rushed in, struck the side of the boat, nearly capsizing it while simultaneously filling it with water. Then the skiff jerked free and floated, complete with a soaked and yelling Thomas, out into the harbor. Miraculously he was able to stay on board and the boat didn't capsize. One of his oars and several floorboards floated away while he began frantically bailing. Then, once the errant oar had been plucked out of the water, he rowed away from me without a backward glance, toward his all-consuming hope and longing on the other side.

Alone on my little island, I could only stand and watch him go.

Winslow Homer (1836-1919) "The Gale". Ca. 1883

CHAPTER TWENTY-FOUR ~ KILA

The two most important days in your life are the day you are born and the day you find out why.

—*Mark Twain*

I grew accustomed to slaughter. We had to kill many animals on our little farm and while I never enjoyed it, I didn't hate it either. It was a necessary part of our life, and I became proficient at removing skins and organs from creatures hung upside down from rafters. Thomas would always be the one to shoot the larger animals in the head with his .22 pistol, but I killed the chickens, first by chopping off their heads and later by slitting their throats. The birds would go into a docile state while hanging by their feet and this was how I positioned them before the final goodbye. The geese had more goslings that we killed, plucked, and roasted. The male goat kids were butchered when just a day or two old, so we wouldn't have to feed them our milk. They dressed out at about the size of a large cat, but the meat was mild and delicious. We also had lots of small pigs we had to kill, since there was no market for them on Monhegan and we couldn't afford to feed them all winter.

I attempted gardening, but the sod was tough and the soil shallow. Very little grew during these dismal trials. Since Thomas had a Mainer's dislike of almost any vegetables he did not encourage the gardening endeavor. When we finally pulled down the old rotted sheep barn below our house, I fenced the area where it had stood and planted a garden in the foot of composted sheep manure that was left behind. My cucumbers were a foot long and the tomatoes huge. I grew marijuana plants that shot up over eight feet tall and my pumpkins were show quality. It was enormously successful, and I was on my way to cultivating a love of working with soil and plants.

George Bellows (1882-1925) "Breaking Sky, Monhegan" Ca. 1916

Winter was coming again. We dried up the goats by just not milking as often, until they stopped lactating altogether. This was the time of year when we could take trips off the island again. We made a journey to Canada to look for land to buy. Having gotten rid of the VW, we now had an old Chevy pickup truck with a homemade wooden cap on the back that we drove over the border; our marijuana stashed in one of the stake pockets of the truck. Fortunately, the border agents let us drive on through; I imagine our clever hiding place would have been one of the first places they'd have looked. We drove up to Cape Breton Island and a realtor showed us half of a two-hundred-acre island that was for sale, complete with causeway and helicopter landing pad, all for $20,000 US. We didn't have much use for the helipad and Thomas thought the causeway to the mainland was too easy, so we didn't pursue it. He was cooling on the idea of the Canadian relocation by this time so, after one more visit to Nova Scotia the following spring, we shelved the immigration idea for good.

We visited friends of Thomas's in Auburn too. These young people had gone on to be lawyers and professionals; the life-path that their old school chum had taken fascinated them. One such visit found me opening my mouth in front of a group of these people to start telling stories of our life on Manana. Almost of their own accord, out tumbled the stories of Frank and the goat head, Thomas's freezing hands, the attack of the killer helicopter, and the marijuana banana bread. Everyone was laughing, and I was surprised to be enjoying myself. Thomas's appraising look at the end of the evening showed that he, too, was surprised at the change in me; the shrinking violet who never opened her mouth was changing and he wasn't sure what to make of it.

Our fourth winter on the island was when our daughter Kila was born. Once again, we lied to the islanders about her due date and I was grimly determined not to repeat the mistakes of my last birthing. This was going to have to work or I would simply die trying. We invited our friend Sandy over from the mainland near the time we figured the baby was due.

Sandy was one of our long-time acquaintances who stuck with us through all our crazy antics. She and her husband Paul lived in an antique Cape house, complete with outhouse, in Tenants Harbor, and they were a frequent pit stop for us on our trips inshore. Paul was a vintage beatnik in his fifties, with a gray beard, wispy gray hair, and groovy vocabulary. He was a late-stage alcoholic and drug addict from Manhattan, a relic from the 1950s era of jazz musicians, drunken artists, and IV drug users with hepatitis C. Several times Paul convinced me to go into the local pharmacy and sign out terpin hydrate cough syrup for him, so he could get high. He was a sweet man when he wasn't too drunk or stoned, and we were very fond of him.

Sandy was the quintessential New York hippie Jewish mother who always fed us when we arrived, dispensing advice as freely as her food. She was a free spirit in her forties and served as my rock for many years. Thomas and I both felt that she was the only person we could call on to help us deliver our baby and she didn't hesitate to come out.

On the afternoon of January eleventh, Thomas decided to slaughter a buck goat that we had reared that year from a kid. The billy had bred all the does and had therefore outlived his usefulness. We did not keep male goats during the milking season because their musk would taint the milk. Goat milk has a reputation for having a strong odor and taste, but this is due entirely to the presence of the male goat in the vicinity of the lactating does. Without the stinky guy around, the milk was comparable to cow's milk and the resulting cheese was much milder too.

The animal was killed, hung, and disassembled with the usual dispatch as the weather became colder and windier. I was feeling a little tired that day and had been having false labor pains on and off for weeks. I was sitting inside resting when Thomas presented me with a bowl with two glistening round objects about the size of golf balls quivering in the bottom. "Rocky mountain oysters!" he exclaimed, and asked me to cook them up. So, I did, and we had them as a snack before dinner. Soon thereafter my waters broke, and labor started in earnest. Later we joked that those testosterone-laden goat balls chased that baby right out of me.

This labor lasted less than six hours. I had set my mind on keeping control and under no circumstances was I going to panic again. She was a big baby, much bigger than Orca had been, and I tore when she came bursting out. But out she came, on a cold blustery night in the middle of the winter on our tiny island in the middle of nowhere. She is, as far as I know, the only baby ever born there, and will likely retain that distinction forever. This infant had the funniest face: all squished looking, but her eyes were mine. At the tender age of nineteen, I was now the mother of two.

Orca slept through it all but the next morning he was at my side, trying to figure out where this little squealing thing came from. He immediately tried to poke her eyes out, but I knew he'd get used to her in time. I named her Kila (KEE-la, rhymes with Gila), because I thought it was a sweet name for a sweet baby.

Thomas's only comment was how *ugly* a baby Kila was. It was true; she was a little funny looking. We dressed her up in her finest a couple of days later and brought her across the harbor to meet the world. One island lady came forward and after gazing at Kila's bald, lopsided

228

head and squinty eyes, she finally said, "Oh, what a beautiful…
sweater."

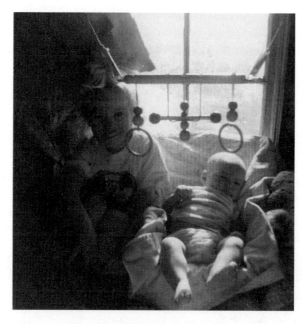

Orca and Kila on Manana

Kila was an easy baby. She had none of Orca's temper and
fussiness; instead she just glided through her life with open-eyed
wonder and a sweet smile. Everyone fell in love with Kila; that was just
the way she was. Orca viewed her as a cross between a toy, a
companion, and a pain in the ass. They developed a deep bond, those
two, at a very early age and while Orca constantly teased and tortured
his sister in as many ways as he could devise (and they were countless),
they both depended heavily on each other as the years went by.

Now I had two children to shepherd across the harbor. Orca was
old enough to sit on the seat of the skiff by himself and I would bundle
up Kila in a backpack. By that following summer she was crawling and
leaning out of her pack to smile and drool at anyone who would look at
her. She charmed them all.

Another summer was upon us, our hands were very full, and we
were both getting a little tired of our routine. The goats had multiplied,
and we had many to milk twice every day. Thomas took a job on a seine
boat that summer. This entailed him spending the whole night out on the

water and then crawling home dead tired in the early morning while I desperately tried to keep the kids quiet while he slept all day. Of course, that's impossible with an infant and two-year-old, so he frequently exploded into rages, telling us all to "shut the fuck up!" I took to taking the kids off the island as often as the weather and tides allowed.

Kila on my back

If I knew anything at all, it was that I was not going to have any more children. Two were plenty for me and I went about trying to make arrangements to have my tubes tied. I had turned twenty that spring but found out that in order for Medicaid to pay for my sterilization, I had to be twenty-one. I found myself stocking up on condoms and spermicidal jelly; taking extreme care to make sure that birth control measures were strictly followed, because I knew that I was done having children. I had enough to deal with without more kids.

CHAPTER TWENTY-FIVE ~ ISLAND IN DECLINE

Sex and drugs and rock and roll
Is all my brain and body need

—*Ian Dury & The Blockheads*

W e'd mail-ordered a hundred day-old Khaki Campbell ducklings and were raising them to be egg layers. Dozens died because we didn't have the proper brooding facilities for them, but over half survived to become the loudest quacking demons imaginable. Every morning at dawn they'd start in: QUACK, quack, quack, quack, quack. QUACK, quack, quack, quack, quack... until finally one of us staggered out of bed and threw some food at them. Then the goats would wake up, baaaaaing and baaaaaing until we were ready to feed and milk them. The donkey would chime in with his incredibly loud braying and the geese would squawk and honk. The pigs would grunt and squeal for food and the roosters had to compete with one another for the top crowing awards. Old McDonald had nothing on us and it was becoming a terrible responsibility to care for all these creatures. We soon found ourselves looking longingly across the harbor toward Monhegan, where there were parties and people our ages hanging out and having fun and no barnyard animals.

We started drifting across the harbor more and more, skipping a milking here and there, just not caring about it anymore. During one of our longer absences the goats broke into the grain room and the more dominant nannies devoured as much grain as they could stuff down. This resulted in a deadly bloat and three of them died terribly painful deaths as a result of our neglect and their gluttony. I felt horrible about it.

Thomas's roving eye didn't go away but I made sure to stick close to him. This way I managed to foil any attempts at extracurricular activities on his part. He flirted with lots of girls, but they had to get by me first and none of them tried. I was becoming a little more assertive in my old age (hell, I was twenty now!) and could even stand up to Thomas once in a while. Slowly, I was changing from the wraithlike, semiformed being I'd been into something a little more substantial.

George Bellows (1882-1925) "The Harbor, Monhegan Coast, Maine" 1913

I found that I enjoyed going to the island parties or schoolhouse dances more and more; we'd leave the sleeping kids at the Summer

Cottage, usually unattended, and go whoop it up. I'd tell myself that I'd check on them periodically, and usually I would. I grew to love a glass of wine in the evening, which quickly turned into two or three glasses of wine in the evening. I could drink prodigious amounts of beer, and would do so whenever I could. I found that I could drink more than Thomas, since he had a very low tolerance for alcohol. In fact, I could drink many men under the table. Thomas would comment on my drinking from time to time, but I just figured he was being a jerk. Of course, we always had marijuana to smoke—that was a staple in our lives and definitely Thomas's drug of choice.

It was 1979 and by this time, younger island residents began to have bigger and wilder parties, and more and more folks were getting involved in drugs and alcohol. One of the richer summer residents introduced cocaine to the island and its highly addictive nature hooked many, including my in-laws. I was fortunate to be too broke to dabble much in that seductive drug. Also, since I found that snorting coke had about the same effect on me as a couple of cups of strong coffee, I just didn't get into it. Our friends Tim and Marie became heavily involved. They began trafficking cocaine and other drugs to help support their habit; making regular trips to New York City, buying dope to bring home and sell back on the island.

Islanders began experimenting sexually as well, with several couples getting together from time to time for an evening of spouse-swapping. There were even reports of orgies, which is not something you hear about every day. This made for some very interesting gossip, but the end result was that long-term relationships on Monhegan began to dissolve and the divorce rate on the island skyrocketed.

Thomas decided to curtail our partying. The behavior of the islanders was shocking even him; I think he was afraid that I would get sucked into it in a way he couldn't control. While I didn't have any interest in the sexual stuff, I really didn't want to give up partying either. It felt so good to laugh and be with people and I loved to dance. It became another struggle between us. I felt trapped on our little island with my babies and intolerant husband, when all I wanted to do was go out and have a little fun. I took to bringing home a large bottle of wine every day and discreetly polishing off as much of it as I could each night. It seemed to help somehow.

FLAT ASS CALM

CHAPTER TWENTY-SIX ~ SINSEMILLA

Life is just one damned thing after another.

—Elbert Hubbard

We cruised through another summer on Manana. The days were growing shorter and the seas rougher. Kila was taking her time about learning to walk but she was a good crawler and could zoom around on her hands and knees like a little dynamo. Her hair sprouted out blonde and curly; she was adorable.

Kila and Orca

235

Orca would go between loving his little sister and torturing her. Kila's first words were, "OR-TA, NO!"

One day my sister Irene wrote and asked if we were interested in a short-term job out in California. She and her husband owned a small house and a few acres in the foothills of the Sierra Nevada Mountains near a small town called Nevada City. On this land Irene was going to make her fortune growing killer marijuana. She needed someone trustworthy to help her bring in the crop when it matured. We were offered an hourly wage unlike anything we had ever seen, so we decided to go out and do it.

We arrived in an early-1980s California whose government actively engaged in a war on locally grown drugs. The foothills of the Sierras were a patchwork of marijuana fields and the local, state, and federal authorities were well funded to hunt them all down. Irene's garden wasn't overly large, less than a quarter the size of a football field, but her marijuana plants were huge—about ten feet tall and covered with the precious sinsemilla buds. That California climate certainly did agree with them, and Irene's green thumb was ten times bigger than mine.

My mother Dora was living near Irene at the time in the little town of Rough and Ready. This was our first visit to California and we had to manufacture some excuse for this trip that didn't include illegal activities. So, we told my mother that Irene's husband had given Thomas a job doing carpentry. Dora was glad to see us and although she and Thomas circled each other like wary dogs, we managed to spend some time with her. She had come to Monhegan a couple of times to visit us since I had left home, but this was her first meeting with Kila and she was charmed.

We moved into Irene's house and nervously watched the plants get bigger and more mature. When the buds were fully developed, the plants would need to be cut down and hung to dry. Each bud would then be carefully removed, trimmed of all the little leaves, and packaged in Baggies to be sold for some outrageous price. Most of the THC was stored in the bud, and the price for good sinsemilla was very high. Of course, we had to sample the wares often and were constantly stoned while we were there.

The reports began to come in of raids in the nearby hills; huge trucks loaded with soldiers with M-16s and dogs, crashing down gates and hustling the growers off to jail before burning the fields. These raids were usually heralded by an overflight of a spotter plane to identify the site. This did not help the feeling of paranoia that settled like a thick, unpleasant smell on us all. I was scared shitless.

Finally, Irene's nerve broke, and she announced that we would cut the plants down and hang them upside down in the woods to dry under sheltering branches where they couldn't be seen. We hustled up to her hilltop garden and began chopping at the thick trunks of her beautiful plants. A misty fog had settled over the area and the plants were wet and springy. We tied them up on lines strung between the huge Douglas fir and were immensely relieved when it was finally all done. The fog lifted that afternoon and we watched in horrified amazement as a small plane appeared and began to circle the now-empty field. It was the spotter plane. We had no idea if they would follow up with the raid or not. We fervently hoped that since the field was bare they would leave us alone, but we still had over a hundred plants hanging like laundry under the trees and we were all very vulnerable.

We began to process the crop in Irene's basement, all the while keeping an ear out for the unmistakable sound of trucks crashing through gates. I had devised a plan to grab the kids and just head into the woods if anything happened. My naive assumption that I could run for the hills and be safe helped keep me from going crazy with fear. We worked, sweated, and started to get on each other's nerves. Irene and Thomas were both dominant personalities that needed to be in charge, so they soon began bickering. After a particularly nasty fight, Thomas decided it was time for us to leave. Since we hadn't finished the job, we didn't have much in the way of earnings, but I was never so happy to leave a place in my life. Soon we were back home on Manana, preparing for another winter.

FLAT ASS CALM

CHAPTER TWENTY-SEVEN ~
TOXOPLASMOSIS

There is nothing permanent, except change.

—Heraclitus

A few months after our California trip, in late winter, I was standing on the wharf watching the mail boat come in, with all the usual activity that accompanied this three-times-per-week event. I was gazing across the harbor at the little island of Smutty Nose and noticed that the outline of that little island seemed blurry. My vision had always been excellent, but it had suddenly changed. Unsure, I blinked. Still blurry. How odd. I looked around and noticed that my vision seemed different somehow. There wasn't the clearness that I'd always had before, and I couldn't figure out how this could have happened so suddenly.

My father had moved to Maine and was living in Camden. I called him from the island store and asked if he knew of any eye doctors in the area. He found me an ophthalmologist in Rockland. I trundled my babies in with me on the following boat and found myself sitting in a waiting room decorated with NRA posters, declaring our right to bear arms. Thomas would approve of this place, I thought.

The office was busy—there were mostly old folks there—but the doctor, who was no spring chicken himself, was kind and spent a lot of time looking in my right eye. Something definitely wasn't right—there was a strange-looking *thing* in there and I had two blind spots where there should only be one. He wasn't sure what the problem was but ordered blood tests. They came back positive for toxoplasmosis; I had a tiny parasite lodged in my eyeball that was slowly growing and screwing up my vision.

There was immediate concern about my children because this is a scary disease for kids, so I had to hold them both down for blood tests too. They were not pleased. Fortunately, they both came back negative and I was started on a treatment of drugs and steroids to remove the parasite from my body.

Toxoplasmosis is a nasty little critter that is usually picked up by humans via cat's litter boxes. It can also be found in almost any animal's feces; since I was in very close proximity to about ten different types of animals, it was anyone's guess where it came from. In pregnant women, it almost always causes miscarriage and it can sometimes migrate to the brain with pretty horrendous results.

Manana and the Harbor

That winter became the winter of endless trips to the mainland for my weekly eye checkups and progress reports. I had dye injected in my veins and photographs taken of my eye. Lots of ophthalmologists in

240

the state wanted to see my rare disease and me. I weaned Kila before going on my medications and my breasts at long last began to dry up. The parasite was eventually killed off with treatment, but I had to wear glasses after that.

I stayed with my father in Camden on my trips inshore. Although Al could not abide Thomas at all, he still welcomed me into his lovely big Victorian house on High Street. His home became yet another haven for me. He did get a little miffed the time I borrowed his big Dodge van while he was away and used it to transport goats... but he got over it.

There was a bar in Camden called The Garage. There I took to meeting island friends who were also marooned on the mainland, and we would all get roaring drunk together. One night I met up with my friend Marie, who was on a shopping trip off island and we became two girls out on the town together. It was then that she confided to me just how bad things were getting. Her life was completely out of control: she was horribly addicted to cocaine, had become almost skeletal in appearance, and couldn't stop drinking. Her husband was becoming abusive to her and was seeing other women. She was on the verge of either dying or getting out and I became very afraid for her.

The outpouring of misery that she shared with me that night was almost overwhelming. When we parted she begged that I never let anyone know about her downward spiral. I had confided in her my worries about my own marriage and Thomas's attempts to see other women, so we were bound in a pact of secrecy.

My doctor brought up the subject that maybe my living conditions were not the safest for my children and me. Both of my parents and Thomas's parents started, as a united front, to actively lobby us to leave Manana.

When it finally got through to me that exposure to toxo could be devastating for Orca and Kila, resulting in brain damage and other horrors, I told Thomas that I was not going to live on his little island anymore. After much argument and resistance, he reluctantly agreed, and we packed up and moved into his family's old Summer Cottage that winter. My four-year sojourn was finally over, and I would not return to Manana to live.

Manana Silhouette

It was hardly surprising that Thomas would never forgive me for shattering his lifelong dream.

PART IV

FLAT ASS CALM

CHAPTER TWENTY-EIGHT ~ BACK ON MONHEGAN

If you're going through hell, keep going.

—Unknown

The Summer Cottage required some work to make it habitable during the winter. We insulated the walls, covered the windows with heavy-gauge plastic sheeting, and banked hay bales around the open crawl spaces underneath. The copper water lines had burst, and Thomas taught me how to solder them back together, so we could have a functioning water system.

The cottage occupied the space formerly taken by the old Monhegan House Inn's pumphouse and there was a freshwater well of grand proportions in the backyard, covered by a deck. I designed a gravity feed water system consisting of a fifty-five-gallon drum perched in the eaves of the cottage to which a hand pump was attached. This allowed us to pump water from the well into the drum, from where it ran into the house plumbing system, resulting in hot showers and a flushable toilet. Unfortunately, the first freeze seized up the water line that was shallowly buried between the house and the well and it stopped working. We had to bucket water from the well into garbage cans in the house, then pump it into the drum. Not as easy a task but still effective.

245

This was the first time we'd had running water in five years and I thought it was the ultimate luxury.

Thomas made daily trips across the harbor to feed the animals until we were finally able to get permission to fence off some land owned by our old employers, Doug and Harry, to hold the beasts for the winter. We got rid of Jacques the donkey and sold many of our goats and sheep to Sandy and Paul. A chicken coop was constructed in our backyard for the biddies, so we still had our fresh eggs.

Thomas spent a great deal of his time chopping wood for the stove. Since Monhegan did not have much in the way of hardwoods, we burned lots of green spruce that year. One night I looked out the window and was amazed to see the whole world lit up with a bright orange glow. Wow, I thought, that sure is pretty… until I realized that the glow was the sign of a raging chimney fire… in *our* chimney. We hustled outside to see the little Summer Cottage chimney issuing forth huge red flames like a blowtorch. Large, flaming sparks spewed forth, were caught by the wind and whisked off over the hill. It was very impressive and fortunately no damage was done but we learned the hard way the result of burning creosote-rich wet softwood. But because we couldn't afford to buy hardwood, we just took care to clean the chimney more often.

The Summer Cottage was not the most uplifting place to spend a winter. It was cramped and smoky inside. The overboard sewer pipe was prone to freezing, making the use of a chamber pot a necessity most of the winter—not a pleasant prospect with Kila in toilet training, especially when Orca once tipped it over when full. It was still better than Manana though.

To keep busy, I set my loom up in the living room, and began to weave some clothes for the craft store to sell the next summer. The stitch and bitch crowd of Monhegan women had started a craft shop that year, which provided an outlet for all those sweaters we knitted. While I was on Manana, I taught myself (through books, of course) how to shear a sheep, card the wool, and spin it into yarn. Our sheep were all black and brown animals, so I never bothered with dyeing the wool. We had also purchased some Angora goats, whose soft, curly wool spun into beautiful mohair. During our first winter back on Monhegan, we found an old loom for sale inshore and (once again through books) I began to educate myself on the intricacies of weaving. It was an absorbing and interesting process and I enjoyed it. My creations were pretty rough with a real homespun look, but they were liked by the tourists and sold well in the shop.

Edward Hopper (1882-1967) "Blackhead, Monhegan". Ca. 1916-1919

It was now 1980 and (to use a weaving analogy) the warp and weft of Monhegan's social fabric continued to unravel. In a last-ditch effort to save herself, our friend Marie packed up and left her husband and the island to go live in New York City. She joined AA and began the long difficult process of trying to piece her life back together again. Other marriages on the island were breaking up as well, and the population plummeted from the 125 residents of the mid-1970s to less than half that number. Wild parties continued with feverish intensity. The older islanders began to grumble about how out of control things were becoming, even making threats of barring some of the more outrageously behaving fishermen from the lobstering fleet.

While everything seemed to be falling apart around us, Thomas and I seemed, perversely, to be drawing closer together. We had settled into a routine of married life that seemed comfortable and somehow easier. After we moved back to Monhegan there was one awful episode where Thomas's beating of Orca almost landed our little boy in the hospital, and this near-disaster seemed to scare Thomas enough that his physical abuse of the children, and me, finally stopped. He seemed to be cooling on his pursuit of other women too, and I was able to convince myself that horrible phase was over.

In his more depressed periods, Thomas still blamed me for our banishment from Manana. He reiterated many times how important he'd felt when he lived over there, how he was considered a special person as Manana's hermit, and now he was just ordinary. I could only shrug my shoulders and wait for these times to pass, which they always eventually did, allowing me to once again convince myself that nothing was wrong.

My drinking continued with several beers or glasses of wine consumed each evening as a matter of course, and our use of marijuana was as prevalent as ever. Alcohol use was just a way of life on Monhegan. To not drink was unthinkable. I never attended a party without getting drunk. I loved booze, and while I always had a slightly uncomfortable feeling that I might be following my mother's footsteps, I was able to justify *my* drinking as being totally under control.

One day we heard from our old friend Sandy that her husband Paul had gone into the VA hospital near Augusta for drug and alcohol treatment. We were relieved to hear this because Paul really did have a problem and our trips to their home were becoming less frequent due to his increasingly erratic behavior. Soon he was back home and the daily AA meetings they both attended to keep him sober dictated their lives. Sandy became an expert on substance abuse and treatment and would talk endlessly about it, while we politely listened. Marie was also very vocal about her progress through the AA program in New York and, while we didn't pretend to understand what all the fuss was about, we became vaguely aware of a strange new entity that was just starting to come on the scene, known then as the recovery movement.

The week after I turned twenty-one I checked into the hospital in Rockland to have a laparoscopic tubal ligation. Thomas flatly refused to have a vasectomy. He was absolutely convinced that the operation would keep his penis in a permanent state of flaccidness. I had never regained any desire to have sex with my husband since my first pregnancy, and I had no illusions about my libido being able to sink any lower than it already was, so I undertook the feminine version of sterilization surgery for myself. I returned to Monhegan the next day, groggy from the anesthesia, and finally free of the looming threat of pregnancy in my future.

George Bellows (1882-1925) "The Gulls" 1911

That summer I went back to working at the Monhegan Store during the evening hours, when Thomas could watch the kids. Doug and Harry's drinking had continued its inevitable course to the point where it became evident that the two of them were pretty much sharing one brain cell. Since running a business was getting in the way of their drinking, they finally decided to sell the store to a couple from the mainland, who took over the business in short order. Soon I was back at my old job, working the cash register for the new owners, while furtively sipping beer from a Coke can.

FLAT ASS CALM

CHAPTER TWENTY-NINE ~ THE BAIT BAGGER

Love never dies a natural death.
It dies because we don't know how to replenish its source.
It dies of blindness and errors and betrayals
It dies of illness and wounds;
It dies of weariness, of witherings, of tarnishings.

— Anaïs Ninn

During the late summer of 1980 we noticed the presence of a new young woman who had made it known that she intended to stay on the island for the winter. She was a tall, spirited brunette with long, muscular legs, the result of having bicycled from Wisconsin alone that summer. She came to Monhegan on a whim during her journey and instantly fell in love with the place. Soon she made our acquaintance and Brenda began hanging out with us. She found a winter rental not far from our home and began to line up bait-bagging jobs to carry her through the winter.

Bagging bait had become staple winter employment for women on Monhegan. Unlike mainland fishermen, who generally bagged their bait as they fished, the islanders preferred to have all the day's herring ensconced in their net pouches before setting out each day. Winter fishing does not lend itself to stuffing partially frozen fish into bags while on a wildly rocking boat with the frozen spray in your face. It was far more efficient and less smelly for the fishermen to pay some poor minion to hunker down in the fish house with a little kerosene heater to bag the bait for them. Fast baggers could earn a pretty good wage and there seemed to be no shortage of this work for anyone willing to stink like a rotten herring all winter. After doing it once or twice, I avoided it like the plague.

Fish houses on Fish Beach (Penobscot Marine Museum)

There were two young men who came to the island every summer, both of whom I had secret—*very* secret—crushes on. One was a tall rough character named Chuck and the other was a short, balding Italian guy I'll call Mike. Chuck represented the wild, rebel-without-a-cause type, smoking unfiltered cigarettes, playing guitar, drinking with abandon. Mike was more the smooth Latin lover who would flatter a woman and work his way, very successfully, into bed with her. Mike and Chuck were close friends and would often visit us to share a drink and a joint, play music with Thomas, laugh, joke, and sneak glances at me. I was flattered by the attention and let my crushes flourish in secret, but I had to be very careful not to let anything show. On the outside I was the perfect wife, but I always wondered in my most secret mental realms what it would be like to sleep with another man.

We still went to parties; Thomas was reluctant, but when I finally explained that I was going to socialize with or without him, he usually came along to keep an eye on me. The typical Monhegan party was a pretty predictable affair. There was usually a keg of beer or two, a full bar consisting of rum and Coke and... Coke and rum, a few munchies (but nobody was really there to eat anyway) and lots of music and dancing.

If I hadn't left school at the age of sixteen to live on Monhegan, I would likely have become a dancer. I'd loved dancing since I was a child and I could cut up the floor with the best of them. I wasn't a dancer of the prescribed steps like the waltz and foxtrot, and never cared much for dances you had to learn, like line or contra dancing. I was a wild, free-spirited dancer, allowing the music to completely take me wherever it dictated my body would go. Thomas was a good dancer too. Together we could put on quite a show. Dancing was the only time I felt completely free; I loved a good dance party like nothing else.

It was at one of these parties, when Thomas had gone home early, that Mike actually propositioned me. It was the very first time since being with Thomas that another man had openly told me he wanted to sleep with me. I hastily declined the offer; there was no way I would endanger my marriage and I knew without a doubt that any sort of infidelity on my part would be the end of life as I knew it—everything would be kaput, over and out. Cheating on Thomas was simply unthinkable.

Another winter was staring us in the face. We'd sold off all the goats and we only had left a couple of sheep left on their own on Manana, our chickens, and of course the Alice the wonder dog. All of our friends left for the season except for Brenda, and she took to coming down to our house every night to smoke dope, play music, and keep us company. She had lots of stories to tell about her trip across country. She had taken out a student loan and used the money to buy a bicycle and camping gear and then set out on her own to discover America. I was very envious of her gall, and while her stories of sleeping with almost every man between here and the Midwest gave me some pause, I thought she was a very interesting and courageous woman.

Brenda was the recipient of much island attention. Attractive, unattached females were rare indeed, and there were lots of horny sternmen and dissatisfied husbands who constantly vied for her attention. She rebuffed them all and it wasn't until late winter that I realized the reason for this restraint on her part. She already had her eye on one man in particular—Thomas. She had been coming on to him for weeks and Thomas had tuned in almost immediately. I was just so supremely confident that all was well now, with no more clouds on the horizon, that I had completely missed the greatest threat of all.

One night, just before the onset of early spring, we were invited to Brenda's house for dinner. Since I was tired, and the kids needed to be put to bed, I left early. When Thomas didn't come home that night I knew that my carefully tended, fragile world was finally about to come crashing down.

I always had to give Thomas points for honesty—even when what he had to "honestly" relate to me was so hurtful that I felt it was tearing me in two. Lying and sneaking would have been much easier to deal with at the time. He told me that he was now in love with both Brenda and me, so it would be best if he just went back and forth between the two of us, in order to keep everyone happy. Somehow this didn't seem like a workable solution, and I don't think Brenda was too keen on it either, though I never actually got around to asking for her opinion.

There was the inevitable crying and weeping on my part and the intractable determination on Thomas's part, the end result being my decision to move out. Moving out while on Monhegan presented some difficulties. There were no winter rentals available and I had no money. I called my older siblings, the owners of the Vaughan House where I had spent my childhood summers, and got permission to stay there.

The Vaughan House, that old antique cape cottage (read: no insulation) was situated directly in a wind tunnel of the coldest blasts of arctic air imaginable. It was cold there… no, that's not entirely true… it was unbelievably fucking freezing there. I had to pull my cot directly up to the stove that was stuffed full of wood, cranked as high as it would go, and I still froze all night. This was despite loads of blankets and me wearing a full set of flannel clothes, complete with hooded sweatshirt with the hood pulled tight over my head and only my nose and eyes peeking out. I put the kids in a double bed together under a mountain of blankets and quilts that would have suffocated an ox. They fared better than I did, partly because they had each other to keep them warm. Why I put up with this and didn't kick Thomas the hell out and make him find some ice cave of his own is beyond me. I suppose this act was my big statement: I was now an independent woman and damned if I was going to let on to anyone that it wasn't easy.

Vaughan House, ca. early 1900s (Ellen Vaughan collection)

I can say with supreme confidence, having been through it twice now, that separation and divorce suck. As a rule, it is a unique experience where all parties involved display the least amount of sanity possible and I was certainly no exception.

When begging, pleading, and groveling didn't work to get Thomas back, I tried the other tried and true tactic: sex. I wore alluring clothes and put out tons of pheromones as I paraded my wares shamelessly in front of my wayward husband whenever I could. While he obligingly took me up on my offers of sex, he didn't change his mind about Brenda.

I would sit home in my cold Vaughan House, drinking glass after glass of wine, envisioning my husband locked in a steamy embrace with that… slut. One windy and freezing night I simply couldn't stand it anymore, so I stumbled out into the storm and soon found myself back at the Summer Cottage, shamelessly peeping in the windows of their living room to catch them in the act. Thomas spotted me immediately and threw open the door to confront me. I was only able to babble some nonsense before I lunged back out into the darkness toward my rightful home. It wasn't a pretty picture and after that ugly scene I left them alone. The fact that I had almost completely imitated my mother's insane behavior may have escaped me at that time, but I did know that I had sunk way below my normal level of pride. I'd hit a particularly humiliating emotional bottom and it was time to start clawing my way back up again.

My last-resort means of lashing out and retaliating was by finally sleeping with another man. I took a trip to New York, ostensibly to visit friends and seek some refuge in that wild and crazy city. It just so happened that Mike, the smooth Latin lover who'd propositioned me the year before, was living upstairs in the building where I was staying. Before I was there two days I was sharing his bed and erasing my past with Thomas forever.

Having sex with another man was a very scary experience. I was shy and skittish and had no idea what to expect. But it turned out to be garden-variety sex as usual and the mystique quickly wore off. I found out very soon that Mike really wasn't my type. So, after only a few days I bolted from him and New York, returning once again to Maine.

When I got back to Monhegan I made haste to throw my little affair in Thomas's face. He'd come over to the Vaughan House to visit (and likely to see if any sex was forthcoming). I noticed he'd taken up smoking cigarettes and now reeked of tobacco. When I told him I'd slept with Mike he was enraged by my betrayal and told me that we were truly finished and that he would never touch me again. My emotions of loss and triumph warred with each other as I watched Thomas storm off, but one thing I knew for sure was that our relationship was finally and truly over.

Often in those days I would walk alone for hours on Monhegan over trails and headlands, through solemn firs, and along slippery rocks caressed endlessly by monotonous waves. I'd sit on a cliff, towering over a relentless ocean, lost in the complexities of my troubles, but mostly feeling very sorry for myself. It was during one of these periods of solitude that a kind of perspective came into my life. When I compared the magnitude of the sea to the insignificance of my predicament, my problems became less. The fact that I was now on my own suddenly began to look like an opportunity instead of a curse. For the first time I felt a tiny fragment of peace.

Orca and Kila at the Vaughan House

Of course, our rending in two had a major effect on our children... mostly Orca. He was present during a few of his parent's screaming fights and it frightened him horribly. Kila responded mostly by bedwetting and delayed toilet training, but she was still only two. Orca was four and more susceptible to damage. He began acting out and getting into trouble whenever possible. He cut all of his and Kila's hair off one day, stole money from me whenever he could, painted the walls in the Vaughan House in his own creative fashion, stole the keys to an islander's truck, and generally became a major nuisance.

One day he swaggered into the Island Spa gift shop and demanded about a dollar's worth of penny candy. Old Zimmie, the proprietor, figured something was up when Orca slapped a twenty on the counter for payment. Zimmie smoothly took the twenty, telling Orca that this was the right amount and later, with a wink, gave me back my stolen money.

Kila

Needless to say, there were no secrets on the island about how my kids were behaving, nor about how I was neglecting them. As summer approached I would shoo Orca and Kila out of the house to have a moment's peace from their incessant demands and hyperactive energy. I was simply not able to deal with my kids along with everything else. While under my care they became little waifs on the island, wandering around from house to house, usually semi-clothed or fully naked, and cared for by anyone who would take them in. I was too obsessed with my own problems and finding work enough to put food on my table to notice or to care. Ultimately, I was ill equipped to handle my children by myself because there was still too much of the uncared-for child left in me. I had miles to go before I would be ready to assume all the awesome responsibility required of being an adult parent. Later Thomas and I took to sharing the kids; one week with me and one week with their father gave me a little breathing room and I was able to step up into a parenting role again.

It's with a lot of sadness and regret that I look back on my poor parenting skills. I well remember how my mother's neglect had shaped me, and I was completely unaware of how faithfully I was perpetuating that generational dysfunction.

FLAT ASS CALM

CHAPTER THIRTY ~ ON MY OWN

Loneliness is the poverty of self; solitude is the richness of self.

—*May Sarton*

My long-suffering mother Dora came to Monhegan to stay with me in the Vaughan House the summer after Thomas and I split up. I think martyrdom suited her because she seemed to think nothing of closing up her house, paying rent to her older kids who owned the Vaughan House, and making it possible for me to stay on.

Of course, my price for this was enduring the inevitable "I told you so" implied or expressed by any mother who finally has the sweet chance to show that she'd really known what was best for her daughter all along. I could only grimace and bear it.

Dora had changed quite a bit after I left home. She seemed to live more for her children than for her own wants and needs. She called and wrote us often, listened to our tales of woe, and always offered whatever assistance she could. I honestly think she had many unexpressed feelings of guilt about how her actions had affected her kids and she seemed driven to make amends. She had mostly sworn off the alcohol, with only occasional relapses; however, she was still depressed. After many, many attempts, she eventually managed to quit smoking later in life. Her main occupation was buying older homes and remaking them into well-designed, beautiful living spaces before she became bored with them and moved on. That and her many books and love of reading kept her going. Her boyfriend Nels was with her off and on during her travels, until he succumbed to bone cancer in the mid-1980s, leaving her bereft; she remained single for the rest of her life.

Orca took on his grandmother in his usual fashion, challenging her every move and attempt at discipline. He was experimenting with various forms of verbal insults at the time, many of which would make a sailor blush. During a particularly angry moment, while being told by his Grandma to do something he didn't want to do, he screwed up his face and came up with what he thought was the most horrendous insult of all,

"You, you… MUDFACE!" he screamed at her.

Having already been called lots of less complimentary and unprintable things by her grandson in the past, Dora responded to this outburst with a gale of laughter and for years after she would always sign her letters to me: Love, Mudface. Or just Mud for short.

Dora's arrival was of enormous help to me because I had finally shifted my focus away from getting Thomas back and toward surviving on my own. I was also completely broke and since the kids spent equal time with Thomas and me, he saw no reason to contribute a dime to my upkeep. I had to get a job, so I decided to try house painting. It seemed to be a good choice; there were lots of houses on Monhegan endlessly in need of paint and it was a job where I could set my own hours and work at my own pace. The fact that I had only lifted a paintbrush to paint a skiff or two was not, I thought, an issue worth worrying about. I borrowed a ladder and put up signs around town calling my new business "Off the Wall Painters." I advertised that I was in business in the best way I knew how, by painting the front of the Vaughan House in full view of everyone. Slowly the jobs started to come in.

I had to learn a lot of little survival things, like how to open a checking account of my own and manage a checkbook. While actually balancing a checkbook seemed beyond my abilities at the time, I found if I just put a little more money in than I took out, I could manage. I had to learn the hard way that sending cash to the bank by mail was not wise.

Life on Monhegan was pretty simple anyway; there were no utility companies to contact or other big hassles to deal with. I would simply buy a bottle of LP gas when I needed one, pick up a little kerosene for the lamps, keep up with my store tab, and that was it. I really didn't think that I could make it on my own forever though, and waited impatiently for the right guy to come along to rescue me.

Me on the wharf (1981)

Summertime on an island is a great time for romance and I didn't have long to wait. Chris was the son of one of the island's summer artists and he had come out to pay his father and stepmother a visit. He was a very cute guy in his mid-twenties with dark blond hair and an infectious smile. His own marriage had broken up a few years before, after he and his wife tragically lost a baby to stillbirth. His wife's resulting grief was so overwhelming that the marriage could not survive; she left with another man.

I really liked Chris. He was funny, smart, very sexy, and loved to take pictures. It was with Chris that I learned that I could actually enjoy sex again. Chris fancied himself to be an intellectual (my mother audibly scoffed) and had socialist leanings. We got along splendidly, and he was good to the kids. He also had experience painting houses, so we went into business together and he taught me everything he knew about it. We worked well together, but when fall loomed he decided he couldn't stay. I was heartbroken and begged him to reconsider but there was nothing on Monhegan for him. He was a child of the city and returned to New York.

Dora had left the island by that time. She felt like a third wheel when Chris was around and soon after she purchased a home in Bath. I also realized that my time in the Vaughan House was running out soon; I had to seek a home somewhere else on the island for me and my kids.

It never occurred to me for an instant to leave Monhegan and go back to school, or try to make a living elsewhere. Monhegan was my home forever and I wouldn't leave without a spitting fight. I sought out every owner of every house I could think of and was turned down by them all. I guess Orca's experiments with abstract expressionism on the Vaughan House walls made me a poor risk as a tenant. Thomas and Brenda were making plans to spend the winter in Tucson and the kids were going to be left with me.

Thomas told me in no uncertain terms to stay out of the Summer Cottage—that was his turf and I had every intention of complying with his wishes. While we had formed a somewhat uneasy truce over the course of the summer and were able to talk about issues concerning the kids, I still avoided him as much as possible, and did what I could to prevent an outburst of his ever-present temper. If he wanted to take his little hussy off to Arizona with him that was just fine with me—the farther away the better as far as I was concerned.

Orca turned five in August of 1981 and started kindergarten at the one-room Monhegan School the following month. During his first day at school he bit the teacher and climbed out the window to make his escape. His schooling experience basically went downhill from there. Over the course of that first year the teacher, a neophyte right out of teaching school—like all of Monhegan's teachers—begged me repeatedly to remove my son from kindergarten to give him another year to mature.

I knew that the teacher very likely wouldn't be around next year and I felt he was just trying to make his own life easier at the expense of mine, so I refused. Word had trickled back to me that one of the island's more responsible residents was threatening to call the state and report my children's lack of supervision. I was becoming very aware that there was no way that I was going to be able to keep an eye on my troublesome son all the time, so school was where he was going to stay. In hindsight I now realize that another year to mature was actually the better choice for Orca, but I wasn't able to understand this at the time.

Fall was in the air when an ex-boxing champion moved in with me in the Vaughan House. Margie was a big, handsome black woman with a crackling wit and a mouth full of southern drawl. Formerly known as Margie K.O., she had once held the title of woman's welterweight champion in the early 1970s. Margie had come to Monhegan on the arm of another woman but had gravitated to another friend of mine in short order. Margie and her new girlfriend were crazy about each other and since they had no place to stay I invited them to move in with me in the Vaughan House.

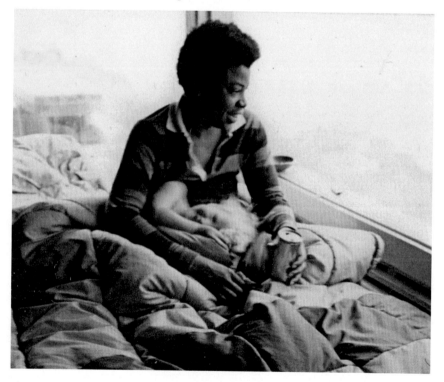

Margie and Kila

We had quite a time that autumn, us three. Margie drank more than anyone I knew (a considerable amount indeed). She couldn't seem to start her day without a beer and a joint for breakfast, which even I thought was a bit excessive. She had a little girl of her own who was about Orca's age and we all got along well together.

After our friend Marie left the island for good, her husband Tim was quickly becoming a persona non grata with the fishing community due to his increasing dependence on cocaine and the consequent insanity of addiction. He entertained (in the biblical sense) several women that summer; along with all the other shenanigans taking place in island society, it was a great soap opera to watch and offered some much-needed distraction from my own somewhat syrupy drama. I was still painting houses and figured I had almost enough money to last through the winter, provided I could find a place to stay. I was still having a bit of trouble finding a winter home, but I kept my fingers crossed that sooner or later, something would come my way.

CHAPTER THIRTY-ONE ~ BAD COMPANY

Always acknowledge a fault.
This will throw those in authority off their guard
And give you an opportunity to commit more.

—Mark Twain

I still missed Chris. I would wander down to the store to place long, lovelorn phone calls to him in New York, pouring my heart out and weeping. The phone cable to the mainland had broken for its final time that year and the Coast Guard announced that they would no longer fix it. Somehow, they had assumed responsibility for providing phone service to the island in years past, but it had become too great a liability for them. To deal with the crisis, island committees were formed, the Maine Public Utilities Commission was contacted, and implementation of true telephone service for Monhegan was underway.

To placate the restless natives, New England Telephone installed a radiotelephone at the store to be used free of charge by all the islanders until the details of installing a microwave system could be worked out. It was on this phone that I whispered sweet nothings to Chris and recited in great detail fondly remembered details of our sex life, never realizing until much later that everyone on the island with a VHF radio could— and did—tune into that frequency and listen avidly to my fascinating, lurid true confessions.

Sonny began knocking on my door right around that time. I'm not very proud of my relationship with Sonny, the reason being that I succumbed to some of my lower instincts when I took up with him, namely fear of being alone and broke. Mostly it was due to the fact that I was getting truly frightened that I wasn't going to find a place to stay that winter. Sonny happened along right at that vulnerable moment in my life and offered to put all my troubles to rest. Who the hell he thought he was kidding, I don't know; it certainly is not to my credit that it took me a few months to catch on that he was not the answer for me. I can be a tad slow at times.

Sears Gallagher (1869-1955) "Broadway, Monhegan" Ca. 1940s

Sonny was much older than I, about twice my age in fact. He came from an old Monhegan family, going way back to the beginning of time, when one old fellow named Trefethern owned the whole island. Sonny's mother June was one of the more notorious drunks on the island. She had, in her time, been a good-looking, hard-drinking island gal who went through husbands like paper towels. Sonny was the first child of her first marriage. That marriage lasted until a second brother, Peter was born and then fell apart, due, most likely, to June's drinking.

Sonny soon left the island with his father, but his younger brother stayed on with June.

Sadly, Peter went on to become a career criminal, spending most of his adult life in prison. June herself would marry three more times—including twice to the same man—and she had two more children living on the island, as well as an adopted grandson.

The summer I was living in the Vaughan House, June had one of her famous "Yard Sales." These consisted of her lugging a bunch of her belongings out to the yard to be placed on tables, all ostensibly for sale but with no prices evident. Once an unsuspecting buyer was lured onto her yard, he soon found out that nothing was actually for sale at all; this was just a big ploy to get people to come up and visit. If the disappointed customer had the gall to insist on trying to buy something, June would proceed to yell insults at him until he left. Since she lived directly across the street from the Vaughan House, this display provided endless hours of entertainment for us.

Up until this point, I never really knew Sonny; he rarely visited the island and I was never introduced to him. Hence it was with some bemusement that I surveyed June's eldest son one day standing on my doorstep and nervously asking me out on a date.

"A date? Where on earth can you go out on a date on Monhegan?" I asked in disbelief.

This seemed to stump him for a second. Then inspiration struck, "How about the Trailing Yew?"

The Trailing Yew was one of the older, seedier lodging establishments on Monhegan. It consisted of several decrepit buildings grouped together in a compound where a visitor could have the pleasure of renting a very basic room with very basic meals and sharing his bathroom with about twenty other very basic folks. It was cheap, though, and it had a large following of people who returned year after year to partake of the basicness.

The Yew was lorded over by Josephine Day, an ancient lady in her eighties who carefully did herself up each day with lots of pancake makeup topped off with an improbably dark brown, slightly singed, lopsided wig. The wig was burned during some prior mishap involving the cookstove. Jo Day usually could be found sitting in her rocking chair in the Trailing Yew kitchen, instructing her help on how to throw a codfish into the oven to be baked to death and served at the communal dining table. This bland fish dinner usually included canned peas, mashed potatoes, and a salad: a small chunk of iceberg lettuce decorated with half of a canned peach. It was hardly gourmet fare, and the food's tastelessness was only made worse by the torture of having to share it with a bunch of clueless tourists who, once word leaked out that you actually lived on the island, would hound you endlessly with questions about island life: Does it snow in the winter? How much? How do you go back and forth to the mainland? Is there a school? How many children? How many year-round residents are there? ... The whole experience was about as fun as a root canal so why on earth I accepted Sonny's offer of a date to that august establishment remains a mystery to me to this day.

I closed the Vaughan House door in a daze after I had so foolishly accepted Sonny's invitation.

"What da hell did *he* want, Amers?" demanded Margie. She always called me Amers.

"He asked me out to dinner at the Trailing Yew," was my faint reply.

"You goin' out with *him*??"

"I guess so," I said weakly.

Margie just shook her head sadly. I'm sure that she believed that my IQ had immediately plummeted to the minus numbers.

"Don't, worry," I said, "I can handle this."

Dinner at the Trailing Yew was every bit as horrible as expected, even when I tried to lighten things up a bit by explaining with complete seriousness to the table-full of gape-jawed tourists that the way the trucks were *really* brought out to the island was by waiting until the ocean froze in the winter and driving them out. I was well lubricated by that time with all the cheap wine that Sonny had brought along to oil the hinges of what would be a very squeaky start to our relationship.

270

Sonny mostly just stared at me like I was a goddess on a half shell. He sputtered and seemed unable to get two words out when asked a simple question, like why on earth he'd asked me out to begin with. He wasn't a bad looking fellow; handsome in a somewhat gone-to-seed way. He'd made a success of his life, first becoming an airline pilot, then the owner of a marina in Rhode Island. He drank like a fish, smoked like a chimney, and was not very articulate at all. He made sure to let me know that he had just accepted an offer on his marina for over a million bucks and was looking for the girl of his dreams to settle down with. For some bizarre reason I, the hippie-dippy Manana goat lady, seemed to fit this criterion. I was completely baffled as to why.

I tried at first to resist him. He was too old, too conservative, not at all my type, and I didn't want to have anything to do with him. But he was persistent and every time I looked around, there he was, giving presents to me and my kids, offering me flowers, and making a general nuisance of himself. So, I gave in. I took a little trip with him to see his marina in Rhode Island.

It was a big spread and looked well run and managed. Sonny showed me into his upstairs apartment. While I eyed the many conflicting patterns of wallpaper on the walls, including a particularly tasteful rendition of *Pink Panther* cartoons in the bathroom, he spruced himself up by slapping on a gallon or so of Old Spice cologne.

Finally, he was ready to escort me to his bar. The marina had a bar on site and it turned out that this was where Sonny spent an awful lot of his time. We went down and had a few drinks and Sonny got so excited to have me there that he actually fell off the barstool. After that his legs weren't working very well and I had to support him in our trip back to the apartment, where we collapsed on his satin sheets.

I really don't know what in the hell happened but for some crazy reason I was agreeing to move in with him off the island. Before I knew it, he had procured an apartment for us in Port Clyde on the mainland for the winter. Margie and her girlfriend left the Vaughan House in disgust, and I packed up the kids and myself to take a stab at inshore living.

I am happy to report that things did not last long between Sonny and me. He was sulky, uncommunicative, hypercritical, and quickly turned out to be an even more impossible son-of-a-bitch than Thomas. He drank constantly, even when driving, and once when we were on our way home from a long session at a bar, a deer darted out in front of his truck. I cried out and Sonny hit the brakes. The truck skidded and slammed the animal off the road so we pulled over and I got out of the truck. Sonny watched in astonishment as I took out my knife and slit the dying buck's throat. He was just going to leave the dead creature there, but I insisted we put it in the back of the truck and haul it to our apartment. There I proceeded to butcher the deer and cut him up for the freezer while Sonny watched goggle-eyed. Until that moment, I guess the city boy from Rhode Island had never experienced a true Manana barbarian.

The only thing we had in common was drinking and the amounts we consumed were beginning to worry even me. I put on weight, started have severe digestive problems and one day I finally woke up, looked around me and said, "What in the *fuck* am I doing here?" For once I was able to figure it out before I got too hopelessly entangled. Soon after, while Sonny was away on a trip, I placed a phone call to Thomas's father and obtained permission to move back into the now-vacant Summer Cottage. Orca and Kila were visiting their father for the holidays in Arizona, so the first mail boat run of 1982 found me with all my belongings packed up, heading back to Monhegan and determined never to leave again.

On my mail boat ride back to the island, the captain filled me in on what had transpired on Monhegan just a couple of days earlier, on New Year's Eve. One of the newer island residents, a young man, went completely off the deep end and threatened a young island couple in their home with an ax. Fortunately, no one was hurt, and the seriously disturbed fellow was escorted off the island in handcuffs via special mail boat ride the next day. Since this young man had been living only a couple of doors away from the Summer Cottage, I was considerably relieved that he was gone.

The Summer Cottage was gray and uninviting. I went about trying to make it my home and had soon procured coal for the stove, got the water system going, swept out the dead bugs, and dumped all of Thomas's stuff in the shed. Finally, the house became livable again.

272

Two days later I heard a knock on my door and there was Sonny standing hatless in a snowstorm, asking to come in. I didn't let him past the door and told him firmly to go away and never come back. Fortunately, he obeyed, and I didn't see him again for many months.

Winter on Monhegan is not a very romantic time but I was in luck that January. One of the island wives had just run off with another married lobsterman that fall, leaving her husband behind and bereft. Before you could say, "rebound," the jilted Brad was knocking at my door. I fell hard and fast for Brad. He was the hearty, strong, handsome type in his thirties with thinning hair and a tanned, weather-beaten face. He had formerly been a schoolteacher on the island and had evolved to become a charter sailboat captain in the summer and a sternman in the winter. Brad was Ivy League educated, well-spoken, and I really loved the fact that he was committed to living on my island.

Orca and Kila at the Summer Cottage (1982)

Unfortunately, Brad didn't love me half as well as I loved him and once spring peeked out from the chills of winter, he dumped me like a load of bricks and went on his merry way. Orca and Kila had come back to the island to stay with me that winter and I think the poor man was a tiny bit overwhelmed by my rambunctious children, coupled with my own very needy demeanor. He told me, not unkindly, that he was seeking a more mature lady; I, at twenty-two, did not fit the bill. It took me a very long time to get over him.

I was alone again.

CHAPTER THIRTY-TWO ~ TENDING GARDENS AND PAINTING HOUSES

Experience is one thing you can't get for nothing.

—*Oscar Wilde*

Once spring rolled around, I decided to turn the Summer Cottage's yard into one big vegetable garden. I planned to sell veggies as well as paint houses that summer to support myself and I was making every effort possible to fix up and beautify the cottage as much as I could to ward off any threats of being thrown out on my ear.

Thomas and Brenda had come back to the island and, after a short stint in the same bunkhouse Thomas and I had lived in six years before, they moved back to Manana. Since the animals were finally evicted for good and they had made a concerted effort to clean the place up, Thomas was able to convince me that the children could spend time over there again during the summers. I chose to believe him because the alternative would be him lobbying his parents to get me out of the Summer Cottage, so he could move in and I had no place else to go. I could only count on making about four thousand dollars a year doing what I did and that didn't leave much to pay rent. My friend Sandy had tried to convince me to go on welfare, but aside from taking advantage of any healthcare the state offered, I was determined to make it without government assistance.

Monhegan Summer Cottage (Lorimer Brackett)

I dug up my whole backyard by hand, formed wide beds, and buried dozens of loads of seaweed I'd hauled with our old Garden Way cart from the beach. I strung up an electric fence to keep out the deer and planted many different kinds of vegetables and flowers. The place bloomed and the Summer Cottage had never looked so good. When Thomas's parents came out for a visit, I hired a girl to clean the whole house for them and moved myself out to a friend's house for a few days while they were there. The place looked great and I was a little amazed that I was able to pull it off.

After mourning Brad's departure for the requisite period of time, I found a much more interesting distraction to carry me through the summer. Lucas was a newcomer to the island the previous fall, and had taken a job sterning for one of the lobstermen all winter. He had brought his girlfriend and her little child to live with him, but she departed in the early spring, having decided island living was not her cup of tea.

Lucas was a big guy with shaggy brown hair and beard. He was an ex-Marine Vietnam vet who had seen gruesome activity during the war, including being helicoptered into Cambodia before most

Americans even knew troops were there. He had dealt with his resulting PTSD by getting actively involved in psychodrama, a therapy involving acting out your trauma and reaching resolution through play-acting. It seemed to work for him because during our time together I saw no signs of the horrors currently plaguing other survivors of that dirty little war.

We took up together and I had high hopes that I had finally found the man who would stick by me. I really hated being alone, and was feeling pretty desperate. We began painting houses that summer, and I worked harder at that job than anything I had done before. House painting is not the most mentally challenging occupation out there. It consists of hauling around a lot of heavy stuff like ladders and cans of paint, and scraping soffits and trim until your blood levels of lead are at an all-time peak. I became very good at it and grew to hate it. I could glaze a window with precision, cut in around panes of glass with a brush like a pro, and maneuver a thirty-foot extension ladder by myself. It was hard, boring work, but the pay was good, and I knew I would survive.

My vegetable garden became a success. The seaweed was a great fertilizer and my cauliflower heads were like basketballs. I simply posted a sign inviting anyone to come to my garden between the hours of five and six in the afternoon and I would pick whatever my customers wanted when they showed up. It was a very satisfactory arrangement.

Orca and Kila still ran free that summer. They had their own friends on the island within a year of their ages and their days were spent in playing, mostly unsupervised—as it had always been. Thomas would take them to Manana on his weeks of custody and bring them back and forth across the harbor every day. Kila, now three, was a delightful towheaded child who chattered constantly and Orca at five was the same handsome hellion he always was.

One sunny day they commandeered a skiff, and, with the help of Orca's six-year-old best friend, they were soon seen drifting out the mouth of the harbor. Kila was sitting demurely in the stern holding a very large open umbrella and Orca was attempting to row in a manly fashion. Of course, they weren't wearing life jackets and had been expressly forbidden to take boats out, but that didn't stop them for an instant.

Thomas and I were still not divorced, and the prospects of this happening didn't seem to be anytime in the near future. Thomas was pushing for full custody at first, but once I showed a letter he'd written to me that stated, "…and I don't hit the kids anymore" to my lawyer, he allowed he would compromise with joint custody. I refused to allow him any custody at all, the memories of his treatment of Orca and me in the past being still fresh in my mind. Although there was no evidence he was still abusing his son, I wanted ultimate control over things should he revert back to his old self. We had almost no belongings to fight over; I took the old Chevy Nova, an asset of dubious value. It was a piece-of-shit wreck that required a quart of oil at each fill-up and caused me great anxiety during its mandatory annual inspection—which it never failed to fail. The end result of our impasse was that we settled on agreeing to disagree and went on with our lives, both assuming, correctly, that eventually we would work it out.

The island was constantly abuzz with the latest developments about the upcoming phone service. Lawyers had been hired and consultants consulted. Several island residents had taken the phone service project upon themselves with a single-minded intensity, and it was through their efforts that it finally came about. The ruling came down that New England Telephone was required to provide us little islanders with the same service that all the other citizens in their service area were entitled to. They fought it, of course; the prospect of building and maintaining a full microwave phone system where only a few payphones had previously existed was going to be an expensive burden, and one that they were loath to take on. But take it on they did, and preparations were soon underway to start building a microwave tower at the top of Lighthouse Hill, near the town water tanks. There would be crews to lodge and feed and the prospect of a major distraction that winter was greatly anticipated.

One-day Margie came by and asked me to go look at a vacant island home with her. The owners had been a prosperous fishing family on the island for years, until booze had so eroded their lives that they left their big sprawling island home to seek a new life on the mainland. Their marriage was on the rocks, and they were looking for a way to make use of their old empty house in some income-producing venture. With the phone company storming the island with workers, they hit upon the idea to have someone like Margie run the place as a rooming house to bring in a little money.

Dory at Sunset (with Monhegan light and microwave tower in background)

We went into the big brown house to look around. Margie knew that my mother was an expert at fixing up houses and I was developing an eye for this kind of thing myself, so Margie wanted my opinion of what would need to be done to get this project off the ground. It was a rambling farmhouse with numerous additions tacked on over the years, including a large, incongruous, jerry-rigged swimming pool: a cinder block foundation covered with a plywood roof. I thought the house was really ugly inside, brown apparently being their favorite color. The interior was resplendent with the cheap fake wood paneling and acoustic tile ceilings so popular during the sixties and seventies. The kitchen was large (and brown) with cigarette smoke-stained ceilings and walls, walnut-stained cupboards, and cheap Formica counters. The living room was carpeted with cheap puke green carpet smelling strongly of mildew. There was a bewildering assortment of bedrooms and just two bathrooms, one being a master bath off a large bedroom that was painted a dark Chinese red. It was so dark inside that I needed a flashlight in the middle of the day just to find my way around.

All I could see was the massive amount of work that would be needed to make the place even marginally attractive. The fact that there was only one bathroom, accessible by walking through the kitchen, for all but one of the bedrooms, made it a poor prospect for a guest house. Margie was disappointed but could see my point, so she reported back to the owners; the house was promptly put on the market that fall.

The ongoing social erosion of the island community seemed to be leveling off. Many people had left and in what appeared to be a healthier pattern of renewal for the island, some new ones had come out to stay. The harsh wave of drugs had taken its toll. While drinking remained the most common mode of entertainment, it seemed to be slightly less destructive than the cocaine epidemic had been, and somehow sustainable—after all, rum and fishermen went together like rum and Coke.

My boyfriend Lucas and I would come home after our ten-hour days and relax with a few margaritas to chill us out. Like all my men, Lucas could drink with the best of them, but his drinking hadn't progressed into a problem at that point in his life. Sadly, I would never find out if it ever would become a problem because, come fall, he decided to leave the island. He invited me to go with him, but I never had any intention of leaving Monhegan. I knew that someday I'd find someone to stay with me out there, though I was becoming afraid that this mythical someday might be when I was an old woman. But for the time being, I was determined to stick it out.

CHAPTER THIRTY-THREE ~ A NEW BEGINNING

*Whenever I have to choose between two evils,
I try to pick the one I haven't tried before.*

—Mae West

A long and lonely winter loomed ahead of me. Orca was in the first grade and seemed to be adjusting better to his more regimented life. Thomas was unable to keep the kids on Manana during the school year, so we settled into a routine of sharing the Summer Cottage that winter. I would vacate the house during his week with the kids, then he would move to Manana when it was my week of custody. To accommodate this schedule, I would take trips to the mainland to visit my mother's house in Bath or spend time with my friends, Sandy and Paul.

Sandy was a stabilizing force for me during those years. She never gave up on me, even when she saw the inevitable missteps and blunders that accompanied my chaotic life. My kids loved her; she was like an aunt to them. Sandy would make them cookies and treat them like her own and, when Orca could get away from school, I would bring them with me on our visits.

Rockwell Kent (1882-1971) "Toilers of the Sea" 1907

Alcoholics Anonymous was an important part of Sandy and Paul's lives at that time. They went to meetings as often as they could, and they often repeated AA's guiding principles to me as little tidbits of wisdom. One night while I was visiting, they invited me to a meeting. I was assured it was an "open" meeting that anyone could attend and was instructed that when it came my turn to introduce myself, I could just say, "Hi, my name is Amy and I'm a visitor."

The meeting was in Tenants Harbor at the Legion Hall, and the room was crowded and smoky. I was surprised to find my old neighbor June there. She had moved to the mainland to nurse her last husband to his inevitable death that winter and some well-meaning friend had convinced her to try a few meetings. June never really got AA though, and obviously she hadn't figured out what the second A stood for, because the next day she was calling my father-in-law in Auburn to fill him in on all the details of seeing me at that meeting. I shrugged off this blatant breach of AA conduct because I was only there as an observer and didn't really understand the program too well myself.

I was really impressed by the honesty that came forth at the meeting that night. Here were complete strangers telling everyone in that room about their worst screw-ups, and acknowledging in public what they had done. I was fascinated by the stories and the insight that came out about how to deal with life on life's terms. It was all completely new to me. While I didn't believe I had a problem with booze, I could appreciate the wisdom of this program and how it could help people's lives. Where else could you go and tell a room full of complete strangers what an absolute shit you were and be hugged and kissed for it?

The "higher power" issue was a really difficult one for me and I was intensely uncomfortable with the recital of the Lord's Prayer at the end of the meeting. All forms of organized religion were repugnant to me, being a free spirit and all. I simply couldn't understand why a Christian prayer was used in the setting of people trying to get sober.

While I'm still not crazy about the use of Christianity in AA, I grew to understand that these prayers were just tools. AA was developed in the forties by a couple of drunks with nowhere else to turn. They used what they had at hand—including bits of Christianity, Buddhism, Judaism, and other religions and philosophies—to bring together a moral, practical, and spiritual method of staying sober. The slogans and prayers were meant to be guideposts, not dogma; used for what comfort they had to offer.

Paul told me that he always had a problem with the spiritual aspect of AA too, but he got over it by declaring that his cow was his higher power. Looking at it that way did put it into perspective. It was a revelation to think that I was not superior in any way to cows, chickens, or geese. Like the time that I sat on White Head after Thomas's defection, I was able to fit myself once again into a grander scheme, and recognize that I really was of major insignificance. I finally figured out that I could at last have true freedom only by *not* thinking I was the center of universe.

Despite that breakthrough with the principles of AA, I had not yet figured out that my own drinking might be an issue. After the few meetings I went to inshore, I would return to Monhegan, and fix myself drinks every evening.

Christmas was looming, and I'd decided to stay on the island by myself that year. The kids were going with Thomas to their grandparents and for some reason I'd refused my mother's invitation to stay with her. I was in the mood to stew in my own juices and thought I could handle the holidays without a problem.

This was my first Christmas alone and it was a mistake. I started drinking early in the day "to celebrate" but became sloppily and unhappily drunk before it was half over. After pouring myself the last of the several bottles of "good" wine I had purchased specially for the occasion I began to think I was losing my mind. Tears rolling down my face, I looked at the shambles of my lonely pathetic life and for the first time considered suicide. Was this all there was for me… a lonely existence waiting for the right man to emerge on an isolated island? It was so pathetic that I thought I might just as well just die… from embarrassment if nothing else.

Fortunately, I passed out before I could act on any thoughts of doing myself in. The next day I resolved that I would be a little more careful about how much drinking I did while I was alone and proceeded to put that miserable Christmas out of my mind. I went to the store to call Sandy, inviting myself to their place for New Year's Eve to ensure that I wouldn't be alone that day too. I immediately felt much better.

Sandy and Paul were going out to a New Year's Eve AA dance that night, so of course I went along. AA members hosted lots of social events over the course of the year. The holidays were the worst times for backsliding into drinking, so care was taken to provide alternatives to going out and getting plastered on those special days. New Year's Eve was an especially delicate time for most, so the party planned that year would be very festive and fun. There were over a hundred people there at the church in Rockland where it was held. I was introduced to many new faces and even started to enjoy myself. There was lots of food and after sitting through talks given by members about how great being sober was, the music started up and the dancing began.

Normally I am a big dancer but without the social lubricant of booze I found it daunting to get out on the floor. Everyone there seemed to know everyone else and since nobody knew me, I wasn't even asked to dance. I sat for most of the evening, a wallflower for the first time in my big party career. Finally, Sandy realized my predicament and dragged a young man over to dance with me.

"Bill meet Amy. Amy meet Bill," was our introduction and she pushed us out onto the floor.

There was an awkward silence between us as I surveyed my dance partner. He was a nice-looking fellow just under six feet tall in his thirties, slight but muscular in build with thinning brown hair and blue eyes. His dancing was a little mechanical but that was ok with me as I started to loosen up. The next song was slow, so he drew me into his arms.

"Are you in the Program?" he asked me. This was a standard greeting for anyone who meets a stranger at an AA dance.

"My name is Amy and I'm *not* an alcoholic," I quipped.

He smiled. "What do you do?" he asked.

"House painter." I replied, "And you?"

"I'm a social worker for mentally retarded people," he said.

"Ah," I really didn't know what else to say.

"So where do you live?" he tried again.

"Monhegan," I replied.

"Oh," There was another pause as he thought this over.

Then he finally said with great conviction, "I could *never* live there."

It was midnight. The music stopped, horns honked, streamers flew, and in came the new year of 1983. To my great surprise Bill gave me a big kiss.

Suddenly I knew that my whole life was ahead of me and *anything* was possible.

Sunset Gull on Fish Beach

EPILOGUE

I've looked at life from both sides now
From win and lose, and still somehow
It's life's illusions I recall
I really don't know life at all

—Joni Mitchell

O f course, Bill proved himself wrong because soon after our first dance he quit his job and came to Monhegan to take up life with me for fifteen years. I, for my part, quit the booze and the drugs and spent the next decade and a half attending AA meetings to learn how to live without them.

Bill and I bought the dreary ugly brown house Margie and I had looked at the year before and transformed it into a bed and breakfast. After much hard work, it became a stately home with efficiency apartments and rooms—each with its very own bathroom (yours truly serving as the chief plumber) and beautiful gardens.

Life with Bill was never easy and our lives on Monhegan became even more difficult over the years due to increasing frictions between our claustrophobic island community and us. Many islanders came to resent our big ideas, our drive to succeed, and the fact that we didn't drink. They also showed no reticence in letting us know how they felt in various unpleasant and tiresome ways. While some things changed—namely myself—many stayed exactly the same.

But that's another story for another time.

Orca and Kila grew up on the island, eventually going off to private boarding school when the high school years came. Both kids continued to share their lives with Thomas and me, alternating between the extremes of my workaholic perfectionist partner, Bill, and their laid-back hippie father, Thomas. I saw less and less of them as they got older and when they were finally out of school they both left the island with nary a backward glance, both choosing to live in urban environments for several decades.

When he was fourteen, Orca had a brief stint as a model for Jamie Wyeth; the Farnsworth Art Museum in Rockland has several portraits of my son prominently displayed. Now he's a contractor in New York and is married with two little boys of his own to be tormented by.

Kila went on to live a very different life—living and working in Berkeley for a while, then taking herself off to India, Nepal, and Thailand; she traveled alone for four months, and scared her mother to death. Over the years she has lived in London, San Francisco, and Chicago, and now resides in upstate New York, where she works and attends college.

Both of my children are wonderful people and much to my relief, they survived their rocky childhoods well, in spite of some pretty bizarre parenting.

As for Thomas, Brenda left him early on and he took up with, and eventually married, another woman. They had four children together.

I have no evidence that Thomas continued to be physically abusive to his family. Since we lived next door to each other on Monhegan for several years, I did catch glimpses of his verbal tirades from time to time. I can only hope that his need to physically lash out at others was finally out of his system by the time we split up. People do change sometimes, and I have forgiven, but not forgotten, our tumultuous times together.

Thomas continued to live on Manana, on again, off again, with his new family and soon they began building a house, not far from our old abode. The hermit's shack became more rotted and unsafe as time went by, so one-day Thomas burned it to the ground, thus removing the home of the original hermits of Manana. The rock piles that still dot the surface of that island are all that remain of Ray Phillips' legacy.

I finally, left Monhegan for good after twenty-two long years there. I still have recurring dreams of the island, but they are not happy ones. They're more along the lines of those surreal dreams where I'm back in high school at the age of fifty-eight and am being told that I have to take math for two more years before I can finally graduate and move on with my life. As I said… very annoying.

But the old dreams are fading, as these things are wont to do, and my life marches on… with whole new stories just waiting to be told.

Amy and Kila

FLAT ASS CALM

AFTERWORD

Writing is easy. Fixing what you wrote is the hard part.

—Amy

This book took forever for me to complete. By forever, I mean I worked on it, on and off, for over fourteen years, which seems like forever to me.

I originally completed my first draft of this work in 2003, but my mother insisted that I not publish it before she was dead. I respected her wishes and shelved my manuscript until she died in 2010. Then, after tinkering with it some more, it seemed only fair to wait another four years until my father passed as well. After that, another three years passed before I worked up the courage to drag the manuscript back out, this time for good.

Sometimes waiting is a good thing and I'm convinced this book is far better now than when I first thought it was complete, all those years ago.

Where possible, I have given proper attribution for the photos scattered throughout this book. Many are dug out of our old photo albums of the time or taken by me and a few are from Wikimedia Commons, where they are designated as part of the public domain. I've also obtained historic photos from the Penobscot Bay Maritime

Museum. A big thank you to Abby Sewall for giving me permission to use her photos of us from the book *The Voice of Maine,* by Bill Pohl and Abby Sewall, Thorndike Press, 1983.

I collected all the art photos in my book from Wikimedia Commons. I chose paintings that were indicative of Maine artists during the turn of the twentieth century, including works by George Bellows, Marden Hartley, Winslow Homer, Alice Kent Stoddard, Edward Hopper, Jay Connaway, and Sears Gallagher. Not all of these artists painted on Monhegan, but all beautifully portrayed the essence of the Maine coast.

A huge shout-out to Megan Maxwell for her amazing editing prowess, without which I would never have thought of the hippie Mr. Magoo. That one is all hers.

Finally, I want to thank my husband, Bob, both for his eye for typos and for being my rock over the past twenty years. Of all the fish who have swum in and out of my life, he's definitely a keeper. Oh, and I completely forgive him for falling asleep while reading my book.

ABOUT THE AUTHOR

Amy M. McMullen has lived many places, including New York, Cape Cod, California, Maine, and Arizona. She spent the majority of her life on small islands off the coast of Maine, where she became a small business owner.

Over the years, she has tried her hand at homesteading, property management, real estate investments, home remodeling, and owning and operating two bed and breakfasts. She also did a stint as a boat captain, doing fishing charters and whale and puffin watch excursions. She became an advanced level EMT in the early 1990s and helped create a remote island rescue service.

She is a co-founder of a nonprofit free clinic serving the uninsured in Phoenix, Arizona, which is also the subject of the documentary film, *Salud Sin Papeles/Health Undocumented.*

Her articles on politics have appeared online in *Salon, Truthout, The Tucson Sentinel,* and *Addicting Info. Flat Ass Calm* is her first book.

Amy currently lives with her husband and four dogs in downtown Phoenix.

You can follow Amy on Facebook or Twitter or visit her website: http://amymmcmullen.com.